# PREPARE NOW
## FOR A METRIC
### FUTURE

FRANK DONOVAN

# PREPARE
# NOW

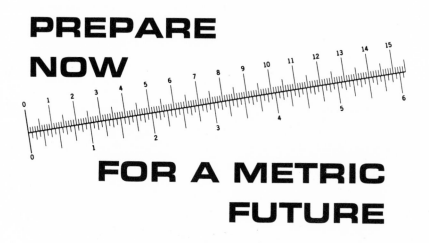

# FOR A METRIC
# FUTURE

WEYBRIGHT AND TALLEY   new york

Published in the United States by
Weybright and Talley
750 Third Avenue
New York, New York 10017

Published simultaneously in Canada by
Clarke, Irwin & Company Limited
Toronto and Vancouver

Library of Congress Catalog Card Number: 71-116527
Printed in the United States of America

BOOK DESIGN BY MILDRED GALLO

*"Weights and measures may be ranked among the necessaries of life to every individual of human society. They enter into the economical arrangements and daily concerns of every family. They are necessary to every occupation of human industry; to the distribution and security of every species of property; to every transaction of trade and commerce: to the labors of the husbandman; to the ingenuity of the artificer; to the studies of the philosopher; to the researches of the antiquarian, to the navigation of the mariner, and the marches of the soldier; to all the exchanges of peace, and all the operations of war."*

—*JOHN QUINCY ADAMS*

# CONTENTS

# PREPARE NOW FOR A METRIC FUTURE

# 1

# A FOOT IS A FOOT—PERHAPS

Shortly after primitive man emerged from his cave to a more social way of life a woman walked to the hut of a neighbor and said, "May I please borrow some mastodon grease?"

"How much?" replied her neighbor.

The borrower, a newcomer to the civilized scene, looked somewhat bewildered and said, "What is 'much'?"

" 'Much,' " said her more sophisticated neighbor, "is like 'some,' but definite. How much 'some' do you want?"

Perhaps the women agreed on a pterodactyl eggshell full, and this became the first measure of capacity. Or perhaps no such conversation ever took place. But it might have, for it is certain that in the dim past of prehistoric days man developed a system of weights and measures as one of the earliest necessities of civilized life.

Even the ancients did not know when or how the metrology that they practiced came into being. The Hebrew historian Josephus attributes its origin to Cain, who built the city of Nod and there conceived the earliest weights and measures. The Egyptians credited their god Theith, or Thoth, as the inventor; the Greeks maintained that it was their god Mercury who deserves the credit. Regardless of where they came from, every civilization of whose early history we have any knowledge had a well-developed system of weights and measures established in prehistoric days.

Linear measurements undoubtedly long preceded units of capacity or of weight since they applied to the most primitive building needs of man. Most experts agree that this form of measurement was in use during the Neolithic or New Stone Age, about 10000 to 8000 B.C., when man was still barbaric, using tools and weapons of flint and stone. As man learned to cultivate the wild grains and developed a communal society the need for measures of capacity to facilitate trade by barter became apparent. Measurements by weight probably did not come into existence until the art of metal working was discovered. Weighing seems to have begun with the measurement of precious metals; no traces of weights or balances have been found in ancient burial mounds until gold in small fragments also appears. The oldest extant weighing device is an Egyptian balance with weights made of limestone that dates from about 3800 B.C.

Experts in metrology—the science of weights and measures—theorize that the earliest linear units were derived from parts of the body. In 1821, at the request of the Congress of the United States, John Quincy Adams, who was then Secretary of State, reviewed the derivation of linear units in a lengthy report that is still considered to be one of the most important documents in the field of metrology.

> The first unit of measures for the use of the hand is the cubit, or extent from the tip of the elbow to the end of the middle finger; the motives for choosing which are, that it represents more definite terminations at both ends than any of the other superior limbs, and gives a measure easily handled and carried about the person.
>
> By doubling this measure is given the ell, or arm, including the hand, and half the width of the body, to the middle of the breast and, by doubling that, the fathom, or extent from the extremity of one middle finger to that of the other, with extended arms . . .
>
> For subdivisions and smaller measures, the span is found

equal to half the cubit, the palm to one-third, and the finger to one-fourth of the palm. The cubit is thus, for the mensuration of matter, naturally divided into 24 equal parts, with subdivisions of which 2, 3, and 4 are the factors; while, for the mensuration of distance, the foot will be found at once equal to one-fifth of the pace, and one-sixth of the fathom.

The use of parts of the human body as well as paces and spans for linear units of measurement is so logical that it is almost certain that the earliest measurements were so derived; although there is no factual confirmation of this. Certainly, the Egyptians believed it; their hieroglyphic for a cubit is the representation of the human forearm.

Women still measure a yard of cloth—the modern equivalent of the ell—by the distance between the end of the outstretched arm and the chin; and horses are still measured in hands—the height of the animal at the withers in terms of 4-inch units, hence a horse that stands 15 hands is 60 inches from his front hooves to the top of his shoulders. Another body-based unit still in use is evidenced by the moderate drinker who stipulates that his tipple be limited to 2 fingers.

The oldest unit of length of which there is literary reference is the cubit. In Genesis, Noah receives divine instruction to "Make thee an ark of Gopher Wood . . . The length of the ark shall be three hundred cubits." All of the civilizations that developed around the Mediterranean used a cubit, or different cubits, thus starting the confusion in systems of weights and measures that prevailed until modern times. Egypt had two cubits at one time and three at another. The oldest was the natural or common cubit of 6 palms. But there was also a royal cubit of 7 palms and, later, a Ptolemaic cubit of a slightly different length. The common cubit seems to have been employed for household use and for commerce and the royal cubit for architecture. The Chaldeans, the Babylonians, the Hebrews, the Greeks, and the Romans each had their own cubits and, while they all measured between about 18 and 23 inches, each was slightly different from the others at various times and in various places.

The use of the cubit in architecture was thoroughly established among the Egyptians by the time they built their first pyramids. The sides of the Pyramid of Khufu, which dates from 2630 B.C., are 440 royal Egyptian cubits at the base with a mean error in the length of the sides of only one part in 4,000.

Although it is logical that the linear foot was derived from the human foot, in some places it was also half a cubit. Two statues of the Sumerian king Gudea, who ruled about 2050 B.C. portray the monarch with a rule in his lap that measures approximately 10½ inches. Gudea was a great builder and it is reasonable to assume that this length, which was exactly half a royal cubit, was then a recognized standard in architecture.

The foot, rather than the cubit, was the fundamental linear unit of the Greeks. Legend has it that the Greek foot was based on the actual measurement of the pedal extremity of Hercules, although there was some difference in the exact length between the units of the various city-states. The length of the Attic foot can be determined from the ruins of the Parthenon. According to Plutarch, the main hall of the temple was 100 feet wide. If Plutarch is correct, the Greek foot used in Athens measures 12.1375 modern inches. To measure longer distances, the Greeks used a pace. A hundred paces equalled a stadium, about 200 yards, and this word was later applied to the amphitheater in which the Olympic foot races were held.

The foot is an excellent example of the regional variation of units bearing the same name that had become commonplace at this early date. There was a Phoenician foot of 10.98 inches. In the Punic colonies of Carthage and Sardinia the foot varied from 11.08 to 11.17 inches. The most common linear unit of the rock tombs of Jerusalem is a foot of 11.3 inches. In the north, the "foot of Drusus," which the Romans used to lay out settlements on the Rhine, was 13.1 inches. This "northern foot," with minor local variations, persisted throughout Germanic Europe well into modern times.

The Roman system of measurement derived something from the several Mediterranean countries that the Romans conquered but, like much of their culture, it borrowed generously from the Greeks. The duodecimal system of numbers was characteristic of the Romans so they divided their foot into 12 uncia, or inches. For longer measures they too used the passus, or pace, of about 5 feet, 1,000 of which formed the Roman mile. As the Roman legions marched through Europe they carried with them their inch, foot, and mile, and these measurements became the common units of most European countries until the development of the metric system. Traditionally, the actual length of a foot in various places was determined by the measurement of the foot of the current tribal chief or other ruler, and the standard might change with the advent of a new chieftain.

As with linear measurements, the first units of capacity probably related to the human body; the handful, or the contents of both hands cupped. This would vary according to the size of the hands of the individual doing the measuring, so some natural object like a gourd cut in half was substituted until the arts of pottery making and basket weaving were developed. Long before village settlements progressed to ordered civilization under dynastic rulers, between 3000 and 4000 B.C., tribal chiefs had undoubtedly set up convenient standards of capacity measurement based on jars, pots, baskets, or skins-full to facilitate trade with other tribes.

The earliest archeological reference to capacity measure is contained in a series of mural paintings, dated 2650 B.C., in the tomb of an Egyptian official. One of these panels shows two series of cylindrical measures, one of copper for measuring wine or oil and the other for measuring grain. In the latter set, wooden "strikes" for leveling off the grain without pressing it down are depicted, the oldest reference to a "struck" bushel.

In his report to Congress, John Quincy Adams described the system of capacity measures of the civilizations around the fertile crescent as follows:

The measures of capacity were, the ephah for the dry, hin for liquid measure; the primitive standard from nature of which was the egg-shell; six of these constituted the log, a measure little less than our pint. The largest measure of capacity, the homer, was common both to liquid and dry substances; its contents nearly corresponded with our wine hogshead, and with the Winchester quarter. The intermediate measures were different and differently subdivided. They combined the decimal and duodecimal systems; the latter of which may, perhaps, have arisen from the accidental number of the tribes of Israel. Thus, in liquids, the bath was a tenth part of a homer, a hin a sixth part of a bath, and the log a twelfth part of the hin; while, for dry measure, the ephah was a tenth part of a homer, the seah a third, and the omer a tenth part of the ephah, and the cab a tenth part of the seah.

Adams picked up this information on ancient measures of capacity from the story of the vision of the prophet Ezekiel in the Bible and attributed all the units to the Hebrews. Later research has disclosed that the homer, the hin (or hon), the ephah, the seah, and the cab (or kab) were also standards of Babylon, Egypt, and Syria, although the similarity of names did not necessarily indicate a uniformity of sizes.

Little is known about Greek and Roman units of capacity because most of their standards were made of pottery and have not survived the ages. The two oldest Greek measures definitely marked as standards date from 550 B.C. and were found in excavations at the Acropolis at Athens. One is a cylindrical corn measure, a khous, which was equal to half the Babylonian log. The other is a water clock marked 2 khous that has a capacity of 393 cubic inches. It seemes obvious that the Greek measures of capacity were taken from those of the older civilizations around the Mediterranean with which the Hellenic states traded. The Greeks merely renamed these units and, when Rome conquered Greece, the same units, with Latinized names, were accepted by the conqueror.

Before commenting on ancient systems of weights, it might

be well to state that the author knows that the use of the word "weight" in this connection is technically incorrect, but follows common practice in using it. The proper term for what is almost universally called a weight is "mass." Mass is a natural property of matter; weight is the measure of attraction between two objects and is controlled by gravitational force. Since the advent of space travel, every school child knows that his weight would be less on the moon than on earth, and that he would be weightless in space; but the mass of his body would remain constant in all three situations. Even the British Parliament falls into the common error of using the word "weight" to indicate a given mass when they officially describe a standard as a "one-pound weight." The mass in question does weigh one pound in the Tower of London; but it would weigh one-half of 1 percent less if taken 10,000 feet into the air or moved to the equator.

The oldest natural units of weight were seeds of grain; principally wheat and rice, although barley was sometimes used. Quantities of gold and silver were measured in terms of the number of grains that they equalled in weight. This was obviously a crude form of measurement since the weight of the grain varied with the type of plant, the lushness of the crop in any given year, and, particularly, the moisture content of the seeds at the time of weighing. A unit called a grain is still a part of the American and British systems of weights and measures. There are 7,000 grains in an avoirdupois pound. The American dollar, which determines the par value of the currencies of all countries in the International Monetary Fund, is equal in value to 15.238 grains of gold.

The oldest man-made unit of weight is the shekel, which equalled about one-half of the modern avoirdupois ounce. This unit apparently originated with the Sumerians, a civilization that preceded that of Babylon on the plain of the Euphrates. The Sumerian shekel standard weighed 129 grains, with local variations ranging from 126 to 132. Sumerian reckoning was on a sexagesimal basis; there were 60 shekels in one mina and 60 minas in one talent. John Quincy Adams again quoted from the vision of Ezekiel in describing the system of weights and measures of the Hebrews: "The weights and coins were the shekel, of twenty gerahs; the maneh [mina], which for weight was of sixty and in money fifty shekels; and the kinchar or talent, of three thousand shekels in both."

The shekel, with variations in mass, was a basic weight and monetary unit in all of the countries of the Middle East. It ranged from 120 grains in Palestine to 218 grains in Phoenicia, with the Sumerian, Babylonian, Assyrian, Syrian, Egyptian, and Persian shekels falling between the figures. It was not uncommon for a country to have two shekels, one as a monetary standard and the other as a commercial standard; or one weight for internal use and the other for the export trade.

The antiquity of the shekel as a unit of weight and a medium of exchange is attested in the Book of Genesis, which says that when Abraham bought the field of Machpelah, "he weighed to Ephron the silver which he had named in the audience of the sons of Heth, four hundred shekels of silver, current money with the merchant."

The Bible also indicates that standardized systems of weights and measures were part of early Hebrew law. In Leviticus is found the injunction, "Ye shall do no unrighteousness in judgment, in meteyard [linear measure], in weight, or in measure [of capacity]. Just balances, just weights, a just ephah, and a just hin, shall ye have." In Deuteronomy it is ordained, "Thou shalt not have in thy bag divers weights, a great and a small. Thou shalt not have in thine house divers measures, a great and a small. But thou shalt have a perfect and just weight, a perfect and just measure shalt thou have."

The Hebrews, in common with other ancient peoples, made the priests the custodians of weights and measures and kept their basic standards of weight and capacity in the temples. These were the official material representations of the various units of weights and measures and were used as prototypes for other standards for commerce and the home.

The early Greek city-states traded widely by land and sea

and apparently used the units of weight that were common in the countries with which they did business. After the Hellenic states were unified through the conquests of Alexander the Great, in the third century B.C., two principal systems were developed side by side in Greece. The Aegina standard was based on an ancient Egyptian shekel, of 192 grains, which was called an Aegina stater. The stater was divided into 2 drachmae, and 50 staters made one mina. The Athens standard was based on a stater of 135 grains and was divided into drachmae and multiplied into minas in the same manner as the Aegina stater. Public standards for reference were at the Tholos in Athens, together with standards of the Daric system for trade with Persia and of the Phoenician system for general maritime trade.

The commitment of the Romans to a duodecimal system of numbers led to the acceptance of the pound as the most widely used unit of weight prior to the creation of the metric system. When they started to coin silver after the conquest of Greece in 268 B.C. the Romans followed the example of the Greeks and other nations and based their unit on an ancient shekel; but whereas the other nations had adopted the various shekels as their coin weights and the mina of 50 or 60 shekels as their larger weight for commercial purposes, the Romans preferred a double shekel for their smaller unit and 12 of these for their larger unit. The smaller unit was an unciae, or ounce; the larger a libra, or pound. Thus their duodecimal system caused the ancient standards on which their weights were based to be submerged and the pound became the unit of the Western world.

As the Roman legions advanced through Europe they found various local systems of weights and measures that, in the interests of trade, it was well to preserve. Instead of imposing their own weights and money, they licensed local mints to issue coinage based on local standards, incorporating this into a duodecimal system on the Roman basis but with the same names for the local units as for those of Rome. Thus there came into being throughout Europe numerous varieties of the

Roman pound and ounce that had little in common except that there were always twelve ounces to the pound. Ancient Roman pound weights that have been found by archeologists vary from 4,210 to 5,232 grains. (The situation had not changed much 15 centuries later. When the mint standards of several Italian cities were compared at the Royal Mint in London in 1819 it was found that the pound of Rome was 5,234 grains, that of Florence 5,240 grains, that of Genoa 4,892 grains, and that of Naples 4,950 grains.

By the time the western Roman Empire collapsed in the 5th century A.D., several systems of weights and measures were well established in Europe. These started as local systems among the tribes before their conquest by the Romans. Then the Roman system was merged with local systems, and, finally, as the Goths moved slowly southward across Europe during the 2nd to 4th centuries A.D., their systems made some contributions.

There was general, but not detailed, conformity among the various systems in European areas that traded with each other. The merchant who bought by the pound from the Gauls and sold by the pound in Rome might not be trading in the same unit in both places but the difference was recognized and was probably no more confusing than the discrepancy that today exists between the British long ton and the American short ton; or between the American gallon and the British Imperial gallon. And it is certain that traders bought heavy in the country and sold light in the city.

None of the systems were, in themselves, entirely logical. Some weights were derived from natural sources, such as grain; others from the weight of water that could be contained in a cube having a given linear side. Some measures of capacity were measures of weight; others were measures of volume —and in some cases the same name might be given to units in both areas. Some units started as one thing and ended as something—or things—entirely different.

Another weakness of logic in some areas of measurement was the tendency to mix two or more systems of numbers in one system of weights and measures. Then, as now, there were four systems of numbers in use at different places and for various purposes: the decimal system in which units are subdivided by tenths, the duodecimal system in which 12 and its factors are the dividers, the binary system of halves, quarters, etc., and the sexagesimal system of division by 60, as in time and angles. The decimal system supposedly came from the Chinese and Egyptians, the duodecimal from the Romans, the binary from the Hindus, and the sexagesimal from the Sumerians and Babylonians.

Many exceptions to the prevailing systems of numbers in various places crept into the systems of weights and measures. The Romans, for instance, used the duodecimal system to divide their foot and pound into 12 units, but changed to the decimal system to divide their mile into 1,000 paces. Such inconsistencies have come down to the present day in England and America. The foot is divided by the duodecimal system into 12 inches, but the inch is divided into halves, quarters, etc., by the binary system—for most purposes. However, in some cases, such as the machining of parts in industry, the inch is divided into tenths, hundredths, etc., by the decimal system. Automobile pistons do not have a tolerance of so many sixty-fourths or one-twenty-eighths of an inch. They are ground to a precision of so many ten-thousandths of an inch.

Confusion in the European systems of weights and measures was well established by the time the Roman Empire collapsed. It was immeasurably compounded during the next several centuries, first by the so-called Dark Ages and then by the period of the feudal system. As with most aspects of culture and learning, the existing systems of weights and measures were virtually lost during the centuries of the Dark Ages when Europe was a turmoil of moving tribes and warring states. In many places, men returned to the "natural" units of measurement that had prevailed before the ancient systems came into being. Once more, a foot was determined by the extremity of a local ruler.

Some parts of the ancient systems were preserved by the Arabs when the Mohammedan Empire rose to power during the 7th and 8th centuries. When their military expansion was completed early in the 8th century, the Arabs turned to the study of more ancient arts and sciences, particularly those of the Greeks. For their basic units of weight they adopted two dirhems: one, for silver coinage, equal to one-third of the Attic stater, the other, for trade, equal to one-quarter of the Aegina stater—units that had originally been derived from shekels. In both systems, 10 dirhems equalled one wukiyeh, roughly an ounce, and 12 wukiyeh equalled a rotl, roughly a pound. The monetary rotl weighed 5,400 grains, the commercial rotl 5,760 grains.

They also had two linear standards; a cubit of 25.56 inches for use in the Persian dominions, and the "black cubit" of 21.28 inches, which was used in Arabia and elsewhere. Each cubit was divided into 2 "feet" and 24 "inches."

At about the turn of the 9th century, Charlemagne reunited much of Europe to create the Holy Roman Empire, which embraced France, the Low Countries, and Germany to the river Elbe. Among many internal reforms that he instituted was an attempt to create at least a rudimentary uniform system of weights and measures. One tradition has it that the standards that he used were sent to him by the Muslim Caliph Harun-al-Rashid—the Caliph of the "Arabian Nights." The *pied de roi* that he created, and that remained the official French foot of 12.7893 inches until the metric system came into existence, was exactly one-half of the Arabic Persian cubit. A more popular tradition has it that the *pied de roi* was the measurement of Charlemagne's own foot.

Charlemagne was the first of many rulers and national governments during the succeeding 10 centuries who attempted to bring order out of the chaos of systems of weights and measures, and he had no better success than those that followed, down to the end of the 18th century. After his death, the countries of the Holy Roman Empire remained united in name only. Real power lay with the feudal lords and barons, each ruling a small section of the area. Every feudal fief and walled city created its own local version of a general system. The people, then as now, had a fondness verging on reverence for old standards; different measures were used for different commodities, sometimes with the same name. A gallon might mean one unit of capacity if used to measure wine and something very different if used to measure oil—and each city had its own gallon or gallons. In linear measures, many crafts had their own units. Cloth was measured in ells, land in rods, horses in hands, depth in fathoms, and printer's type in points.

In most places, there were two independent systems of weights in which units of varying values would have the same names. There was a mint pound and a commercial pound, and materials of great value like precious metals, spices, and drugs were measured by a pound having fewer ounces than the pound that was used to measure more mundane things.

As stronger national governments came into being throughout Europe, successive kings and parliaments sought to bring order out of chaos by making laws to standardize weights and measures in their several countries. This was universally ineffective because the laws did not embrace a total system, they merely sought to regularize parts of what already existed. Also, rulers found that they could fatten the national treasury by debasing the currency, and, when weights and monetary units were related, this created further confusion as to the weight standards.

By the Middle Ages, the number of local units of weights and measures had become almost limitless. The names of many of these found their way into national systems, but they seldom meant the same thing in two places. Until the past century, for instance, the German anker, a measure of capacity, represented 9.07 modern United States gallons in Berlin, 9.57 gallons in Bremen, 9.53 gallons in Hamburg, and various other quantities in every other German and Scandinavian city.

This multiplicity of units continued into the 19th century. In 1850, an American named J. H. Alexander endeavored to compile a record of the world's weights and measures before the metric system, with their equivalents in United States units. His book, which is far from complete, contains more than 4,000 items. Another study, made early in the 19th century, reported, "At the close of the last century, in different parts of the world, the word pound was applied to 391 different units of weight and the word foot to 282 different units of length."

The laws of the Middle Ages governing weights and measures did not go back to the ancient systems. Rather, they sought to regularize, to some extent, the chaos of the Dark Ages. It may be truly said that the systems now in use in the United States and Great Britain are products of the Dark Ages and are inferior in terms of logic and simplicity to the system of the Egyptians 4,000 years ago. The Egyptian system was more advanced in that it took a linear measure, squared it to make a measure of area, cubed it to make a measure of capacity, and then filled the cube with water to make a measure of weight. There was a direct, planned, mathematical relationship between each of their basic units of weights and measures. While it is true that there is a mathematical relationship between our foot, acre, pound, and bushel, the mathematical definition in terms of square feet or cubic inches came after the units were established so that the relationships are arbitrary and awkward.

In the rest of the world, outside of Europe, systems differed but were scarcely more rational, either in ancient times or the fairly recent past. A Chinese traveler wrote of India in the 7th century that:

> In point of measurements, there is first of all the yojana; this, from the time of the holy kings of old, has been regarded as a day's march for an army. The old accounts say it is equal to 40 li; according to common reckoning in India it is 30 li, but in the sacred book of Buddha the yojana is only 16 li. In the subdivision of distances a yojana is equal to 8 krosas; a krosa is divided into 500 bows; a bow is divided into 4 cubits: a cubit is divided into 24 fingers: a

finger is divided into 7 barleycorns: and so on to a louse, a nit, a dust grain and so on for seven divisions until we come to an excessively small grain of dust. This cannot be divided further without arriving at nothingness, and so it is called the infinitely small.

This ancient system may be compared to that which prevailed in Thailand only a century ago. The following table was contained in a school text book in use in the mid-19th century: "One atom equals eight molecules; eight molecules equal one hairbreadth; eight hairbreadths equal one louse egg; eight louse eggs equal one louse; eight lice equal one grain of rice; two grains of rice equal one krabiad; four krabiads equal one fingerbreadth."

The crude systems of the Middle Ages prevailed throughout the world without much question until the 16th and early 17th centuries, when scientists—who were then called philosophers—started to demand something better. In an era when most people lived and died without moving more than a day's journey from their birthplace, the fact that a bushel in Glasgow might differ from a bushel in London had little effect on the lives of the common folk. Traders and travelers could convert from one local system to another and for the rest of mankind the variances made little difference. But the work of the scientists ultimately became international, and science could not progress without an exact, uniform, and invariable system of weights and measures. At the end of the 18th century, scientists created the metric system.

The two principal countries that did not adopt this system, England and the United States, have done much to regularize their own systems in recent years but it should not be assumed that the oddities mentioned herein are relics of a dim past. The ancient Chinese are said to have had two different units called a mile: an uphill mile and a downhill mile. Obviously, since it was more difficult to walk uphill than downhill, the former mile was shorter. Those who smile at this quaint Chinese logic should remember the old riddle that asked which is heavier, a pound of gold or a pound of feathers. Those who sought to demonstrate their superiority by answering that both were equal were, of course, wrong. A pound of feathers is measured by avoirdupois weight and weighs 7,000 grains. A pound of gold is measured by troy weight and weighs only 5,760 grains. However, an ounce of gold is heavier than an ounce of feathers because there are only 12 ounces to the troy pound. When one also considers the two different gallons, bushels, quarts, and pints that are embraced in the Anglo-American system, to say nothing of seven different tons, the quaintness of the ancient Chinese reasoning begins to look like sound logic by comparison. Even a foot is not always a foot: that used by the Coast and Geodetic Survey is based on an inch that differs from the common one by .000005 inch.

# 2

# FROM CONFUSION
# TO CHAOS

Like all primitive peoples, the inhabitants of what would become Great Britain had their systems of weights and measures—several of them. In prehistoric times, the Angles measured in their own peculiar way, as did the Picts, the Saxons, and the Scots; and the Irish had their own inimitable system. When Caesar's legions invaded Britain, the Romans contributed some units; others were derived from trade with the continent. As a result, by the Middle Ages, the system of weights and measures in the British Isles had more varied units than could be found in a like area anywhere else in the world, most of them special-purpose measurements or units peculiar to a specific locality.

If one went shopping and brought home a bind, a bing, a fatt, a flyke, a shid, and a swod, one would unload at the kitchen door 250 eels, 8 hundredweight of lead, 4 bales of unbound books, a side of bacon, 4 feet of firewood, and a bushel of fish. Contrary to the old expression, he would not buy a pig in a poke; wool was sold by the poke and 2 of them were a gybe. It is not clear how much wool made a poke, but 28 pounds of that commodity was certainly a toad and 182 pounds equalled a waga—not to be confused with a waya, which was 336 pounds of cheese.

The ancient English had their nooks and glens but these

were not cozy rural retreats. A nook was a land unit of 20 acres, while a glen was 25 herrings—except in Essex and Gloucestershire where it was a bunch of teasels. A housewife might bring her herrings or teasels home in a maund, a measure whose name survives in Maundy Thursday, the day before Good Friday. Alms given to the poor on this day were traditionally distributed in maunds. And she might buy her corn by the tuffet, a container used as a dry measure. Presumably the one on which Miss Muffet sat was turned upside down. Beer was sold by the bumkyn, wine by the aume or the fust, or, as was hard liquor, by the butt, the pipe, or the puncheon. Butter was sold by the firkin, sprats by the cade, figs by the tapnet, lead by the fother, and coal by the boll or chaldron.

The auncel was a measure of ill repute, for a record of the 15th century states that "Holy Church hath cursed theym that by or sell by that weyght." Some merchants sought to decimalize their transactions by selling a dicker of 10 in lieu of a dozen; a practice that their customers seem to have resented for it brought the word "dickering" into contempt. British florists are today having the same trouble. In line with England's proposed conversion to the metric system, they are offering flowers in units of 10 instead of a dozen, but not all flower buyers take kindly to the idea.

An early English linear measure that became an important unit in the modern system was the Anglo-Saxon yard or gird, which, legend has it, was determined by the length of the girdle of a Saxon king. Later tradition has the yard redefined to equal the arm of Henry I. At the time of the Norman Conquest, the English yard and the French ell were presumably identical; three centuries after the Conquest, official documents in Latin still mention yirga (yard) and ulna (ell) as units of equal length. Later, the ell became a measurement for cloth that varied according to the country of origin; a Flemish ell was three-quarters of a yard, an English ell equalled a yard and a quarter, and a French ell a yard and a half.

The condition of weights and measures in Great Britain became so troublesome that every British ruler from the 10th-century Saxon King Edgar to the 20th-century Parliament has tried to do something about it, without much success during a thousand years of law making. King Edgar ruled that "one and the same money should be current throughout his dominions, which no man must refuse; and that the measure of Winchester should be the standard." A hundred years later, William the Conqueror moved the standards from Winchester to Westminster and repeated "that the Measures and Weights should be true, and stamped, in all parts of the kingdom." In 1225, the Great Charter ordained, "One measure of wine shall be through our realm, and one measure of ale, and one measure of corn, that is to say the *quarter* of London; and one breadth of dyed cloth, that is to say, two ulnae within the lists [between selvages]: and it shall be the same with weights as with measures."

Commenting on these and subsequent rulings, Bishop Fleetwood wrote in the 18th century:

> It was a good law of King Edgar that there should be the same money, the same weight, and the same measures throughout the kingdom, but it was never well observed. What can be more vexatious and unprofitable both to men of reading and practice, than to find that when they go out of one country into another, they must learn a new language or cannot buy or sell anything. An acre is not an acre nor a bushel a bushel if you but travel ten miles. A pound is not a pound if you go from a goldsmith to a grocer, nor a gallon a gallon if you go from the alehouse to the tavern!

A century later, John Quincy Adams said of British efforts to regularize:

> For a series of ages, they have been engaged in the pursuit of an uniform system of weights and measures. To this the wishes of their philanthropists, the hopes of their patriots, the researches of their philosophers, and the energy of their legislators, have been aiming with efforts so stupendous and with perserverance so untiring, that, to any person who shall

examine them, it may well be a subject of astonishment to find that they are yet so entangled in the pursuit at this hour, that it may be doubted whether their latest and greatest exertions have not hitherto tended to increase diversity instead of producing uniformity.

The most oft-quoted law covering British weights and measures is one proclaimed by Henry III in 1266, which provided that

> by consent of the whole realm of England, the measure of our Lord the King was made, that is to say, that an English Peny, called a sterling, round and without clipping, shall weigh thirty-two wheat corns in the midst of the ear; and twenty pence do make an ounce, and twelve ounces one pound, and eight pounds do make a gallon of wine, and eight gallons of wine do make a London bushel, which is the eighth part of a quarter.

The law of 1266 directly connected the weight of money—the penny, 240 of which made the pound sterling—with specific commodities, wine and grain. But the penny had existed before the law was made and is presumed to relate, in a roundabout way, to an ancient shekel. The Saxon King Offa, king of Mercia, is said to have visited the court of Charlemagne where he came into contact with the envoy of Caliph Harun-al-Rashid and was impressed with the beautiful Arabic coinage. Returning to England, Offa had a silver penny coined in imitation of the Arab coins. Because it came from the East it was called an "easterling," which was later contracted to "sterling."

The pound of 240 pence was known as the moneyers pound, or Tower pound, but it ceased to bear a direct relation to commercial weight when later rulers learned that they could inflate the currency by increasing the number of pennies in a Tower pound. In 1344, to pay for the wars with France, Edward III decreased the silver content of the money by coining 300 pennies to the pound.

In addition to the Tower pound there was a merchant's pound, which was one-fourth heavier than the moneyers pound, containing fifteen ounces to the Tower pound's twelve. Edward III sought to have both of these pounds replaced by a third pound; an old French weight of sixteen ounces. The French term *avoir-du-pois* originally applied to the weighing of bulky goods and this expression was applied, with wide variations in the spelling, to the new pound. Edward III ordered that, "Whereas it is contained in the Magna Carta that one Measure and one Weight shall be throughout the Realm of England . . . it is assented that from henceforth one Measure and one Weight shall be throughout the Realm of England." This gave the avoirdupois pound official sanction, but the Tower pound and old merchant's pound continued in use. Then, sometime around 1414, the troy pound was introduced. This pound ultimately replaced the Tower pound, use of the old merchant's pound declined, and England had only two pounds until 1878 when the troy pound was abolished. However, the troy ounce and its division remained and are still in use to measure gems and precious metals.

Even more confusing than the multiplicity of pounds is the British hundredweight. This weighed, as the name implies, 100 pounds until Edward I issued an edict that this sensible arrangement should cease forthwith. In the future the hundredweight would be 112 pounds, except for a temporary period in which it would weigh 108 pounds. Since the British ton was 20 hundredweight, a new long ton of 2,240 pounds came into existence—and still exists.

The ton is another wonderful example of confusion. "Everybody" in the United States and Canada knows that a ton is 2,000 pounds; just as "everybody" in England knows that a ton is 2,240 pounds. Originally, the tun or tunne was an Anglo-Saxon name for a large tub or container. Later, the name was applied to a specific large liquid measure, a unit of 250 wine gallons. This amount of wine weighed 20 of the old hundredweights, hence the short ton of 2,000 pounds, which was *the* ton until the hundredweight was changed. The old practice of buying heavy and selling light prevailed until quite recently in American coal mines, where the pay of miners was based on their production of long tons and the coal was sold to the consumer in short tons.

In addition to these generally known tons, there are the register ton of 100 cubic feet and the measurement ton of 40 cubic feet—these are measures of capacity rather than weight that are used in the maritime trade. The English water ton of 224 British Imperial gallons is used for petroleum statistics in Great Britain. There is a timber ton, which usually means 40 cubic feet, and a wheat ton, which usually means 20 bushels, but the use of these is local and they may vary from place to place. Then there is the metric ton of 1,000 kilograms or 2,304.6 pounds. The word "ton" can mean any one of eight different units of measurement.

To the Saxons, the most important form of wealth in an indestructible form was real estate, and the linear units by which land was measured were more important than weights or measures of capacity. Traditionally, their land measurements were based on the northern foot of 13.2 inches, which was so well entrenched in the Germanic countries from which it came that the Romans had been obliged to use it instead of their own foot when they conquered this area. There were 15 northern feet to a rod (or perch or pole) and 40 rods to a furrow or furlong—a word derived from two Anglo-Saxon roots, "furrow" and "long." The furlong of 660 modern feet or one-eighth of a mile has remained as a popular measurement in horseracing. Other feet were used for various purposes: the Greek common foot of 12.47 inches and the Roman foot of 11.65 inches for building and a "natural" foot of 9.9 inches for some uses.

In 1305, Edward I regularized linear units in The Statute for Measuring Land, by relating the foot to units of grain. This, the most frequently quoted law of English measure, proclaimed:

It is ordained that three grains of barley, dry and round,

make an inch, twelve inches make a foot, three feet make an "Ulna," five and a half Ulna make a rod, and forty rods in length and four in breadth make an acre. And it is to be remembered that the Iron Ulna of our Lord the King contains *iii* feet and no more, and that the foot must contain *xii* inches measured by the correct measure of this kind of Ulna; that is to say, the thirty-sixth part of the said Ulna makes *i* inch, neither more nor less; and five and a half Ulna make *i* rod, sixteen feet and a half, by the aforesaid Iron Ulna of our Lord the King.

Edward's 12-inch foot was apparently a compromise among existing measures, and did not cause too much concern, but Edward could not change the acre—the unit of measurement by which all of the land of England was recorded in the Doomsday Book—so he made up the difference between the 13.2-inch foot and the 12-inch foot by changing the rod from 15 Northern feet to 16½ new feet.

Presumably the acre had been originally derived from the amount of land that a man could plow in a day with a pair of oxen. Edward defined it as a rectangle 40 rods in length and 4 in breadth because it had been common practice in open fields to plow a standard furrow of 40 rods, or one furlong. Later, the acre became any unit, regardless of shape, containing 160 square rods or 43,560 square feet. All of the land in English-speaking countries is measured by this arbitrary unit, which bears no logical relationship to any other unit of linear measure. If an acre is square the length of its side is 208.7 feet.

The mile was probably changed from the Roman unit of 5,000 feet to its present length of 5,280 feet during the reign of Henry VII to make it equal eight furlongs. The first statute describing the modern mile was passed during the reign of Elizabeth I under the title "An Act againste newe buyldinge." After stating that various persons had enclosed, for private use, open spaces around London that had previously been used for the "traynyng or musteringe of Souldiors, or of walkinge for recreacion comforte of her Majesties People," this act prohibited further enclosure "of any of saide Fieldes ly-inge within thre Myles of any of the Gates of the saide Cittie of London." The statute continued, "And that a Myle shal be reckoned and taken in this manner and noe otherwise. That is to saye a Myle to conteyne Eight Furlonge, and everie Fur-longe to conteyne Fortie Lugge or Poles, and every Lugg or Pole to conteyne Sixtene Foot and Halfe."

British measures of capacity were first described in "The Assize of Bread and Ale" issued by Henry III in 1266, which, after saying that a penny sterling "ought to weigh thirty-two grains of wheat from the middle of the ear" continued to re-late capacity measures to weight rather than cubic content: "Eight pounds make the gallon of wine, and eight gallons of wine make the London bushel, and eight bushels make the London quarter." These units were based on the Tower pound but in time they were applied to the heavier merchant's pound. By the time Henry VII came on the scene, the troy pound of 5,760 grains and the new merchant's or avoirdupois pound of 7,200 grains were in use. In 1497, Henry issued a set of Win-chester Standards in which capacity measures were related to troy weight in terms of wheat instead of wine. This edict was the first to define the smaller units; one pint contained 12½ troy ounces of wheat, a quart 25 ounces, a pottle 50 ounces, a gallon 100 ounces, and a bushel 800 ounces.

The confusion about pounds led to the creation of an un-official wine gallon, smaller than the Winchester gallon. This gallon went back to the original specification of 1266, which said that a wine gallon should contain 8 of the lighter pounds. It became so widely used that in 1707 it was legalized (in addition to the Winchester gallon) by Queen Anne by an or-dinance which stated that "any vessel containing 231 cubical inches and no more shall be deemed and taken to be a lawful Wine Gallon." Although most of the English units of capacity were originally related to weight, the later official standards by which they were measured were built to the cubic content of the weight of a given quantity of water.

Since Queen Anne's wine gallon only one important change

has taken place in the British system; a change that served to make it different from the system of the United States in two important areas. In 1824, Britain discarded Winchester measure for what was called Imperial measure. Both the Winchester gallon and the wine gallon were abandoned and replaced with an Imperial gallon that differed from both. The Imperial gallon is a volume equivalent to 277.42 cubic inches, as compared with the wine gallon of 231 cubic inches and the Winchester, or ale, gallon of 282 cubic inches. The Imperial quart was divided into 40 ounces instead of 32. The bushel was redefined to make it the equivalent of 8 Imperial gallons, or 2218.192 cubic inches.

More than 200 years before the Imperial system came into existence, English units of weights and measures had crossed the sea to Britain's colonies in the New World. In common use in America were the inch, which was divided into 10 lines or peppercorns, the foot, the yard, the fathom of 6 feet, the rod of 3½ yards, the furlough of 40 yards, the mile of 8 furloughs and the league of 3 miles. The colonies adopted the Winchester bushel, the wine gallon, and the ale gallon, although the wine gallon was much more frequently used.

Most colonies had standards for the basic measures, but there was little uniformity among them. They had been imported at different times, usually without too much concern as to their authenticity. A few may have been compared with official British standards but this was not always a guarantee of accuracy. Although some of the British standards were surprisingly good, others were no more reliable than a schoolboy's ruler. In 1836, a British metrologist inspected a yard bar from the day of Elizabeth I that, until a few years earlier, had been a standard of the exchequer. He described ". . . this curious instrument, of which it is impossible, at the present day, to speak too much in derision or contempt. A common kitchen poker, filed at the ends by the most bungling workman, would make as good a standard. It has been broken asunder; and the two pieces have been dovetailed together; but so badly that the joint is nearly as loose as a pair of tongues."

A copy of this 300-year-old bar, with impressive parchment documents, had been presented to the United States and lay in a vault in the United States Treasury as a standard for the yard.

Because of the difference in standards, and their interpretation by a variety of colonial regulations, the English colonies in North America had systems that were similar to those of feudal Europe. Although called by the same names, units differed widely in different places. When the United States became a nation, every state used a bushel as a measure of capacity, but none of the bushels was the same. Connecticut's bushel of oats weighed 28 pounds, New Jersey's 32, Kentucky's 33½, and Missouri's 35.

The framers of the United States Constitution recognized the need for a uniform national system of weights and measures. They specified that the creation of such a system was one of the responsibilities delegated to the newly created Congress, which, said the document, "shall have the power to coin money, regulate the value thereof, and of foreign coin, and fix the standards of weights and measures." George Washington, in his first inaugural address, urged prompt action on this, saying, "Uniformity in the currency, weights, and measures of the United States is an object of the greatest importance, and will, I am persuaded, be duly attended to."

The matter of the currency had been considered before the writing of the Constitution. In 1782, Robert Morris, Superintendent of Finance, had written to the President of the Continental Congress "that it was desirable that money should be increased in deciminal ratio, because by that means all calculations of interest, exchange, insurance, and the like are rendered much more simple and accurate and, of course, more within the power of the mass of the people." Two years later, Thomas Jefferson submitted a complete plan of decimal coinage to the Congress with the preface, "The most easy ratio of multiplication and division is that by ten. Everyone knows the facility of decimal arithmetic." Jefferson's decimal system of currency was adopted without much opposition in

1785. An anonymous contributor to the Gazette of the United States wrote, 4 years later, "The Congress division of monies being an exact decimal method, admits of multiplication and division by only placing dots or taking them away. It is the quickest, most certain and easy method of reduction, both for the learned and the unlearned."

In the matter of weights and measures, the first United States Congress again turned to Jefferson, who was now Secretary of State. The Virginian submitted two alternate plans. The first proposed to "define and render uniform and stable the existing system . . . to reduce the dry and liquid measures to corresponding capacities by establishing a single gallon of 270 cubic inches and a bushel of eight gallons, or 2,160 cubic inches." In this he followed the English system, although his units were not exactly the same as either the English gallon or the Winchester bushel.

His alternative system, which he preferred, was "to reduce every branch to the same decimal ratio already established for coin, and thus bring the calculations of the principal affairs of life within the arithmetic of every man who can multiply and divide plain numbers." Jefferson first proposed to define a natural linear unit based on "a cylindrical rod of iron of such length as, in latitude 45° in the level of the ocean and in a cellar, or other place, the temperature of which does not vary through the year, shall perform its vibrations in small and equal arcs in one second of mean time."

Under Jefferson's alternative system, all units of weight and measurement would derive from this linear unit. A foot was related to the length of the second's pendulum and this was to be multiplied and divided in units of ten. "Let the foot be divided into ten inches; the inch into ten lines; the line into ten points. Let ten feet make a decade, ten decades one rood, ten roods a furloung; ten furloungs a mile." The basic unit of mass was to be an ounce that equalled "the weight of a cube of rain water, of one tenth of a foot; or, rather, that it be the thousandth part of the weight of a cubic foot of rain water, weighed at the standard temperature." There were to be 10 ounces to the pound, and a cubic foot of water, which weighed 100 pounds, was designated as a bushel.

Jefferson was familiar with the progress toward the metric system that was taking place in France, where it had not yet been adopted. His system paralleled the French system in its most important aspects, the direct relation of all linear, weight, and capacity units and complete reliance on decimal arithmetic. It differed from the French system in that, in most cases, it retained the old names of units that were familiar to the people. Jefferson's foot would have been slightly shorter than the English foot and his inch somewhat longer, but the new units would have been called by the familiar names.

If Jefferson's plan had been adopted in 1790, life would have been much simpler for all Americans who have lived since, and hundreds of millions of dollars would have been saved simply in the teaching of arithmetic. Congress appointed a committee to study Jefferson's proposal, and this group, after 2 months, reported to the Senate:

> As a proposition has been made to the National Assembly of France for obtaining a standard of measure which shall be invariable, and communicable to all nations, and at all times; as a similar proposition has been submitted to the British Parliament, in their last session; as the avowed object of these is to introduce a uniformity in the measures and weights of the commercial nations; as a coincidence of regulation, by the Government of the United States, on so interesting a subject, would be desirable, your committee are of the opinion, that it would not be eligible, at present, to introduce any alteration in the measures and weights which are now used in the United States.

The Senate saw in this involved prose an excuse for doing nothing, and the legislature continued to do nothing, except appoint committees, for several years, although President Washington continued to remind them of their Constitutional responsibility toward weights and measures. One committee recommended the adoption of Jefferson's decimal plan. An-

other committee proposed the retention of the existing foot
and avoirdupois pound and relating all units of capacity to
these. This was approved by the House but died in the Senate.

By 1799, international trade had become seriously affected
by the multiplicity of standards used at the various ports of
entry in the United States. The rate of import duties was uniform throughout the country but the amount of such duty
varied by as much as 10 percent between cities because each
collector of customs had his own idea of what constituted a
pound or a bushel. To correct this, Congress passed its first
bill dealing with weights and measures, directing that sets of
uniform standards be furnished to the collectors at each port;
a futile act since no set of uniform standards existed. Also,
Congress failed to appropriate any money to make the act
effective.

The United States acquired its first linear standard in 1815
when the Coast and Geodetic Survey ordered from England
an 82-inch brass bar, calibrated in inches, called the Troughton bar after its maker. The divisions on this bar between the
27th and the 63rd were designated as the official yard to be
used in the survey. The mint also needed some uniform standard for coinage, and, in 1827, an exact copy of the British
standard for the troy pound, made of brass, was constructed
in England and ceremoniously delivered to President John
Quincy Adams in a sealed cask accompanied by impressive
documents. These were the only official standards in the
United States.

Meanwhile, in 1817, as the result of one of its perennial
discussions about weights and measures, Congress instructed
John Quincy Adams, who was then Secretary of State, to prepare a report and recommendations. Adams took his assignment seriously and spent four years compiling a book-length
document. He reviewed the history of weights and measures
from biblical times. He studied both the British system and
the metric system in detail. At this time, both the metric system and a system of *mesures usuelles* were legal in France.

His analysis of the metric system was so thorough and so

impartial that, in the arguments about it during the past 150 years, both metric advocates and opponents have used his reasoning to support their opposing positions. Adams favored the metric system for its order, simplicity, and logic. Of it he wrote:

> The single standard, proportional to the circumference of the earth; the singleness of the units for all the various modes of mensuration; the universal application to them of decimal arithmetic; the unbroken chain of connection between all weights, measures, moneys and coins; and the precise, significant, short, and complete vocabulary of their denominations; altogether forming a system adapted equally to the use of all mankind; afford such a combination of the principle of uniformity for all the most important operations of the intercourse of human society; the establishment of such a system so obviously tends to that great result, the improvement of the physical, moral, and intellectual condition of man upon earth; that there can be neither doubt nor hesitancy in the opinion that the ultimate adoption and universal, though modified, application of that system is a consummation devoutly to be wished.

In theory, Adams endorsed the new system, but he questioned the practicality of trying to impose any completely revolutionary system on the people. He pointed to history to support the view that legislation based solely on a desire for order and uniformity had never been effective because

> The power of the legislator is limited over the will and actions of his subjects. His conflict with them is desperate, when he counteracts their settled habits, their established usages, their domestic and individual economy, their ignorance, their prejudices, and their wants: all which is unavoidable in the attempt to change, or to originate, a totally new system of weights and measures.

Adams concluded by recommending to Congress a two-step program: "1. To fix the standard, with the partial uniformity of which it is susceptible, to the present, excluding all innovations. 2. To consult with foreign nations, for the future and ultimate establishment of universal and permanent uniformity." The members of Congress presumably read his report with interest—and did nothing until 1830. In that year, the legislators again became concerned about the discrepancies of weights and measures being used by the customs service, and they ordered the Secretary of the Treasury to make a comparison of the standards used at the various customhouses.

An employee of the Treasury at the time was one Ferdinand Hassler, an ex-engineer and mathematics instructor who had a keen interest in metrology; he had helped John Quincy Adams with his report. Hassler had originally been hired to direct the Coast and Geodetic Survey, but had never proceeded very far with this assignment because Congress kept switching responsibility for it back and forth between Treasury and Navy. In 1830, it was at the Navy and, since Hassler had nothing to do, he was assigned the task of evaluating the standards of weights and measures used by the customs.

As was to be expected, he found that no two standards agreed and so reported to Congress. That body considered his report, appointed a committee, and did nothing further. But Hassler—or his superior, Treasury Secretary Louis McLean —believed that the Constitution gave the Treasury Department the authority to establish standards for the customs, since it provided that customs duties were to be uniform throughout the nation. With no other vestige of legal sanction Hassler set up shop in an arsenal and proceeded to create a complete set of standards of weights and measures for the United States.

For his basic linear measure he took the Troughton yard bar, which he had personally brought from England years before. For his pound he took the troy pound of the mint and constructed a standard for the avoirdupois pound in the relation of 7,000 to 5,760—the difference in grains between the two pounds. By this time England had adopted the Imperial gallon and bushel, but these measures were little known in the United States. For his gallon, Hassler went back to Queen

Anne's wine gallon of 231 cubic inches and for his bushel he took the Winchester measure of 2,150.42 cubic inches, the units most widely used in the United States. The American gallon and bushel were, and still are, 17 percent and 3 percent, respectively, smaller than their British counterparts. They also differed slightly from the old British standards for the wine gallon and Winchester bushel because these were determined by the volume of water at 65° F. whereas Hassler used water at its point of greatest density, slightly over 39°.

Hassler made a set of standards for each custom-house. The avoirdupois weight standards ranged from fifty pounds down to 0.0001 of an ounce—the smaller fractional ounce standards made of silver wire. Troy standards ranged from one pound to 0.0001 of an ounce. He supplied a calibrated yard bar, a standard half-bushel, and a set of liquid capacity measures ranging from one gallon to one-half pint. In 1838, Congress endorsed his work by ordering the Secretary of the Treasury to supply a "complete set of all weights and measures adopted as standards" to the governor of each state, "to the end that a uniform standard of weights and measures may be established throughout the United States." The ironical part of this legislation is that Congress did not first legalize Hassler's standards—they were *adopted* only by Hassler and, through him, the Treasury Department. However, the legislatures of all states that received them were quick to grant them official status so that they became the standards of the United States through the back door, so to speak.

At last, by the mid-19th century, the United States had a system of weights and measures—if it could be called a system. Surely, there was nothing systematic about it. The relation between linear measures and those of weight and capacity were purely arbitrary and, even within a given category, there was no logical relationship between most units. An inch, which had originally been 3 barleycorns, was multiplied by 12 under the Roman duodecimal system to make a foot. Three feet comprised a unit which traditionally had been the length of a Saxon king's girdle. The mile had the odd number of 5,-

280 feet to make it equal 8 furlongs because the furlong had been an integral part of an acre and an acre was sacrosanct to the Saxons.

A duplication of names added to the confusion. There were two pounds, troy and avoirdupois. There were two quarts, one a subdivision of the gallon and the other a subdivision of the bushel, and these bore no logical relation to each other. There were three ounces, the troy ounce, the liquid ounce, and the avoirdupois ounce, which also bore no relation to each other, and, to further confound the user, there were 32 liquid ounces to a quart but only 16 avoirdupois ounces to a pound.

At the time, metrologists did not consider this as a permanent system; it was merely the development of Adams' first recommendation to Congress "to fix the standard . . . to the present, excluding all innovations." Hassler's successor, Professor A. D. Bache, wrote in 1848:

> No one who has discussed the subject of weights and measures in our country has considered the present arrangement as an enduring one. It has grown up with the growth of European society, and it is deficient in simplicity and system. The labor which is expended in mastering the complex denominations of weights and measures is labor lost. Every purpose for which weights and measures are employed can be answered by a simple and connected arrangement.

Meanwhile the metric system had become firmly established as the only legal system in France and was spreading throughout Europe. There was some agitation on the part of scientific organizations for the United States to adopt the metric system and, in 1866, Congress, on the advice of the National Academy of Science, passed a law that provided that "it shall be lawful throughout the United States of America to employ the weights and measures of the metric system, and no contract or dealing or pleading in any court, shall be deemed invalid or liable to objection because the weights and measures referred to therein are the weights and measures of the metric system."

Proponents of the metric system delight in pointing out that the metric system is the *only* legal system in the United States, since the U.S. Customary System now in use was never formally endorsed by Congress. Despite the Constitutional provision that Congress is responsible for weights and measures, this is the only law that the federal legislature has ever passed specifically sanctioning any system. The development of the Customary System now in use has been entirely through state laws and regulations of executive departments of the government.

In 1875, an International Bureau of Weights and Measures, of which the United States was a member, was established in Paris. This body constructed new standards for units of the metric system and presented two platinum meter bars and kilogram measures to the United States. In 1893, T. C. Mendenhall, then Superintendent of Weights and Measures, quietly issued an order, in the form of a bulletin from the Coast and Geodetic Survey, that stated that "The Office of Weights and Measures, with the approval of the Secretary of the Treasury, will, in the future, regard the International Prototype Metre and Kilogramme as fundamental standards, and the customary units, the yard and the pound, will be derived therefrom." By this order, Mendenhall abolished the American standards for the yard and the pound. These units have since been officially based on the French metric standards. Mendenhall's order contained a note to the effect that

Reference to the Act of 1866, results in the establishment of the following:

*Equations*

$$1 \text{ yard} = \frac{3600}{3937} \text{ metre}$$

$$1 \text{ Pound Avoirdupois} = \frac{1}{2.2046} \text{ kilo}$$

A more precise value of the English pound avoirdupois is

$\dfrac{1}{2.20462}$ kilo., differing from the above by about one part in one hundred thousand, but the equation established by law is sufficiently accurate for all ordinary conversions.

Putting it another way, the American yard is not legally 36 inches, it is 0.91440183 meters; the American pound is not legally 16 ounces, it is 0.4535924277 kilograms.

Through the years, comparisons had been made between the British and American standards, which were supposed to be identical. As better means of determining measurement were developed, it was found that they were not. Both the British yard and the British pound had become almost infinitesimally smaller than their American counterparts. The difference was so slight that it had no effect on normal commercial transactions, although there was some slight difficulty during World War II in connection with the interchangeability of airplane parts made to conform to the different standards. In the area of scientific and space calculations the difference was significant. In 1959, the standards bureaus of all the English-speaking countries agreed on a new definition of the yard and pound under which the American yard became by two parts in 1,000,000 smaller than the yard of 1893; it is now defined as equal to 0.9144 meters. The new pound is lighter than the old by one part in 10,000,000.

Because the early Congresses ignored their responsibility in the field of metrology and failed to act on Jefferson's decimal plan or Adams' recommendation for international uniformity, Americans have for almost two centuries been saddled with an utterly confusing and illogical system of weights and measures—which few people understand. Everybody probably knows that there are 12 inches in a foot and 3 feet in a yard; that there are 16 ounces in a pound and 2,000 pounds in a ton; that there 32 ounces in a quart and 4 quarts in a gallon, but universal knowledge probably ends there—and some people remain confused forever as to whether it is the pound or the quart that has 16 ounces. Everybody knows that land is measured in acres, but probably not one person in ten thousand knows what an acre is. Agricultural crops are computed in bushels, but virtually no one knows what a bushel is— which is not surprising since a bushel of corn, a bushel of wheat, and a bushel of apples are entirely different units.

As time has passed, all except the English-speaking peoples have realized the folly of arbitrary and illogical systems and adopted the decimal metric system. The United Kingdom is now in the throes of conversion, and this will leave Americans out of step with well over 90 percent of the people of the world.

# 3
# ENTER THE SCIENTISTS

When Benjamin Franklin retired from his printing business in 1748 to devote himself to scientific experiments, public opinion in Philadelphia strongly condemned him. A man of his ability and attainments should not waste his time fooling around with silly experiments in electricity and writing letters to members of England's Royal Academy. He owed it to the community and to the commonwealth to devote himself to something worthwhile. So Franklin sadly set aside the research that would create the foundation for the science of electricity to lead an expedition against the Indians. Scientists had no standing in colonial America.

In 18th-century England, the scientific fraternity fared somewhat better. The Royal Society had royal patronage, but its findings and experiments were not considered as having much practical value in the affairs of the people and the state. In the western world, France was the scientific cross-roads. Her philosophers and their Academy of Sciences were tendered a certain respect by both government and populace. When the French Revolution created an atmosphere conducive to change and radical innovation, the opinion of the scientists was sought and heeded. Thus was born the metric system.

The basic concept of the metric system was not new in the 1790's. Many who speculated in what would become the sciences had long been distressed by the lack of order, uniformity, and logic in all systems of weights and measures. In 1670, Gabriel Mouton, vicar of St. Paul's Church in Lyon, had proposed a decimal system of weights and measures having a fundamental unit based on the quadrant of one minute of a great circle of the earth. Mouton also related the basic linear unit that would result from his system to the vibrations of the second's pendulum. During the succeeding century, numerous other French scientists came forward with variations of Mouton's system. Their main concern was to establish a "natural" basic unit of measurement rather than the arbitrary toise which then served that purpose in France. A toise, which was 6 French feet, had supposedly derived from half the width of the main gate of the Louvre.

These scientific speculations were only interesting theories until 1790, when a strong and able leader in the French National Assembly, Charles-Maurice Talleyrand, proposed that the Academy of Sciences be instructed to study a universal system of weights and measures for France. Talleyrand suggested as the fundamental unit the length of the pendulum beating seconds at 45° latitude. He was concerned that the new system be truly international and to that end the decree passed by the Assembly stipulated that England should be invited to send representatives of the Royal Academy to deliberate with those of the Academy of Sciences.

If the English scientists received a formal invitation it went unheeded. The French committee spent much time debating the basis for a fundamental unit. Because of their conditioning, the members of the committee were insistent that it have a scientific basis—nothing so arbitrary as a foot or a yard, an ell or a toise. Three units from nature were considered: the second's pendulum, the section of an arc of the equator, and a section of an arc of a meridian.

The second's pendulum—the same that Jefferson was recommending for the United States—seemed the most obvious, principally because it was much easier to measure the vibrations of a pendulum than to survey an arc of the equator or a meridian. But the hair-splitting scientists had two objections to the pendulum. First, it was not universal—the speed of its vibrations depended on its location. It vibrated at a different speed at the equator, where gravitational attraction was weaker, than it did at the poles. Also, the pendulum measurement was based on a second of time, and a second was an arbitrary unit.

The members of the committee decided on a terrestrial arc, which, they believed, was not only uniform but universal. Either the equator or a meridian would do as a basis, and they chose the latter because the equator was harder to survey and, whereas few countries touched the equator, every country was located on a meridian. To determine the length of the meridian accurately they proposed to the Assembly that a survey be made from Dunkirk on the English Channel to Barcelona on the Mediterranean; both cities were on the same meridian and both were at sea level. The linear standard of the new system was to be one ten-millionth of the meridian distance between the pole and the equator as determined by this survey.

Making the survey proved to be a seven-year epic of hardship and frustration for the scientists involved. Following the early stages of the revolution, all of France and much of Europe was in turmoil. Strangers were suspect everywhere, particularly strangers who carried unusual instruments and who put up white flags around the countryside (white was the royal color): the surveyors were undoubtedly secret agents of the Bourbons engaged in some nefarious plot. The survey teams spent some time in various local jails and much more repeatedly explaining what they were trying to do. A letter from one member of the northern party described the troubles that started before they left the suburbs of Paris.

When I arrived at Saint-Denis I had to show my passports and I obtained a permit to remain, but the magistrate warned me that even with that aid I would not travel a quarter of a league. And, indeed, a half-hour after, in passing through

Epinay, we were arrested. They found that our instruments had not been designated with sufficient clearness in our passports; they wished to seize them; I was required to spread them on the ground and explain their use. No one understood the explanation I made, and it was necessary to recommence for each curious person who came. . . . After three hours of debate we were forced to remount our vehicles with an armed guard and were taken to Saint-Denis.

While the survey was being made, a provisional linear unit based on the length of the meridian as determined by astronomical calculations was adopted. This subsequently proved to be little more than one-hundredth of an inch different than the survey distance. One ten-millionth of a quarter meridian —the distance from the pole to the equator—was called a meter; in French, *metre*, from the Greek *metron*, a measure.

There was very little discussion in either the Academy or the Assembly as to the system of numbers to be used in the new system of weights and measures. The decimal system was clearly so superior to any other that it was quickly approved. There was more argument about nomenclature. The Academy proposed monosyllabic names for units, some of them the same as those of the old system. The Assembly, completely logical, decided on polysyllabic names in which Greek prefixes would be affixed to the name of the basic unit to denote multiples of it and Roman prefixes to denote subdivisions. In 1795, an act was passed legalizing the metric system. It provided that

The new measures will be distinguished by the name of measures of the Republic: their nomenclature is definitely adopted as follows:

*Metre,* the measure of length equal to the ten-millionth part of a terrestrial meridian contained between the north pole and the equator.

*Are,* the measure of area for land equal to a square ten metres on each side.

*Stere,* the measure designated especially for firewood, and which shall be equal to a metre cube.

*Litre,* the measure of capacity both for liquids and dry

materials, whose extent will be that of a cube of one-tenth
of a metre.

*Gramme,* the absolute weight of a volume of pure water
equal to a cube of one-hundredth part of a metre, and at the
temperature of melting ice.

The prefixes specified in the act for multiples of basic units
were deka, hecto, kilo, and myria; for subdivisions, deci, centi,
and milli. Thus the linear units were:

| Myriameter | — | 10,000 | meters |
| Kilometer | — | 1,000 | meters |
| Hectometer | — | 100 | meters |
| Dekameter | — | 10 | meters |
| Meter | — | 1 | meter |
| Decimeter | — | 0.1 | meter |
| Centimeter | — | 0.01 | meter |
| Millimeter | — | 0.001 | meter |

Similar prefixes were applied to units of weight; myria-
gram, kilogram, hectogram, dekagram, gram, decigram, centi-
gram, milligram. For capacity, the divisions were kiloliter,
hectoliter, dekaliter, liter, deciliter, centiliter, milliliter. The
only units of area other than the are were the centiare, one
square meter, and the hectare, which equalled 10,000 square
meters.

This was the system that John Quincy Adams described as
"rare and sublime." It had two points of beautiful simplicity.
Its basic units of weight and capacity were directly related to
the fundamental linear unit—the liter was a cubic decimeter
and the gram the weight of a cubic centimeter of water. And
all of its secondary units were multiples or divisions by 10
of the basic units. All one had to know to use the system was
the length of the meter, the relationship to the meter of the
basic units of capacity and mass, and the meanings of the
prefixes. The schoolboy did not have to memorize such arbitrary units as a mile of 5,280 feet or an acre of 43,560 square
feet. The prefix "kilo" told him that a kilometer was 1,000

meters. The prefix "hect" denoted that a hectare was 100 ares or 10,000 square meters.

The Academy constructed a standard for the meter, a platinum bar measuring 39.37008 American inches, the length determined by the survey. Subsequent improvements in the methods of determining terrestrial distances proved the survey to be inaccurate by a significant amount. Quite recent data from the researches of the International Geophysical Year showed that the earth is neither uniform nor unchanging. But by the time that more accurate measurements of the earth's circumference became available the meter was so well established that changing its length was never considered. The scientists who made such a fetish of having a natural basic unit for their system ended up with something that was just as arbitrary as the yard or the foot. Actually, it made no difference. Any unit of a handy length would serve so long as it was basic to all aspects of the system and was divided and multiplied decimally.

The Academy also constructed a platinum standard weight. Although the gram was the basic unit it was too small to represent a suitable standard—less than one twenty-fifth of an ounce. The kilogram, equal to 2.2046 American pounds, was selected as the standard. When these standards were deposited in the Archives in 1799 the metric system became the only legal system of weights and measures in France.

The new system was promptly adopted for scientific work and government transactions in France, but the reaction of the people and the business community was less than enthusiastic. There was much suspicion, resentment, and stubborn opposition. People did not like the long, foreign names of the new units, nor did they understand the prefixes, particularly those derived from Greek. Universal education was not yet widespread in France and communications between the government and the people and the merchants were weak. People had always bought things by the livre or boisseau—the pound or bushel. Their grandparents had lived by these measures. They did not trust the new kilograms and liters. How could they tell whether they were being cheated? Also, political conditions changed when Napoleon became First Consul in the same year that the metric system was legalized. The new government had little interest in reforms effected by their republican predecessors.

The people and most of the business community continued to use the old units of weights and measures. This confusing condition of two systems was legalized in 1812 when a decree was passed recognizing a system of *mesures usuelles* that might be used for retail trade and small business transactions. This was based on the metric system, but it permitted familiar names to be applied to metric units and to multiples and fractions of metric units determined by other than the decimal system. The pied became a third of a meter and was divided into 12 pouce. The boisseau was defined as one-eighth of a hectoliter. The livre became equal to 500 grams, or half a kilogram, and was divided into 16 onces. It was required that scales and measures be marked with both metric and common units and it did not seem to bother most people that the pound and foot that they were now using differed from the old units—so long as they were not called 500 kilograms or 333 millimeters.

Meanwhile, Napoleon, who had relaxed in enforcing the metric system at home, was responsible for the beginning of its spread beyond the borders of France. As his armies conquered most of western Europe they attempted to Gallicize the invaded countries, and this included the compulsory adoption of the metric system. This served to do little more than introduce the nations involved to the new system, which, at the time, was understandably received with resentment.

The first European country after France to legalize the system was Switzerland, where it was adopted by some cantons in 1801—this through the efforts of one of her scientists rather than by force. In Italy, Milan adopted the meter and the kilogram as the basis of a series of measures on a decimal scale in 1803. In both places, the various units were given local names; in Italy the meter became the braccio and the kilogram a libra metrica or metric pound. In Germany, Baden adopted a pfund, equal to a half kilogram, in 1810. The metric system was forced upon Holland when Napoleon invaded that country in 1810, and it was adopted by Belgium when she combined with Holland.

In 1837, France decided that the twin systems that it had been saddled with since the decree of 1812 could no longer be tolerated. The former decree was repealed and the metric system became compulsory as of January 1, 1840. A fine of 10 or 20 francs for each violation was the penalty for those who were found guilty of using other weights or measures after that date.

The real acceptance of the system in other European countries was gradual and took place only after the establishment of more stable governments in the decades following the Napoleonic wars. International trade became more important than military conquest and for the free flow of goods across many borders some uniform system of weights and measures was desirable. In a comparatively small area there were a number of independent states—neither Germany nor Italy were yet unified. Each state had a different system of weights and measures that seriously interfered with easy transactions in international business. Platoons of clerks computed in counting rooms to change from one system to another. To carry on commerce there must be a definite standard of comparison between the goods of the home country and those of foreign origin. Some of the German states led the way by adopting a zollpfund equal to one-half kilogram for their customs, and this quickly spread to the post office departments and railroads of the area.

The upsurge of a general feeling in favor of the metric system in Europe dates from the London Exposition in 1851. Here, after several decades of peace, businessmen from all of Europe came together to display their goods and compare notes. Scientists, statesmen, educators, and economists had long favored the universal adoption of the metric system. Now many businessmen, manufacturers, and merchants became converted. This resulted in the creation of unofficial international committees and associations to consider the subject of weights and measures. In 1870, when the French government invited other nations to a conference to consider the advisability of constructing new metric standards, fifteen nations attended, including Great Britain and the United States. This conference led to the signing in 1875 of the "Metric Convention," a treaty under which an International Bureau of Weights and Measures was established. For its home, France gave the bureau a former royal residence, the Pavillon de Bretauil, in a suburban Paris park, which is still the world center of metrology.

Under the aegis of the bureau an international group of scientists constructed new meter and kilogram standards, making copies or "prototypes" for each of the signatory nations. The United States received prototype meter bars Nos. 21 and 27 and kilogram standards Nos. 4 and 20. These kilograms are still the official standards of weight in the United States, but at an international convention on weights and measures held at the bureau in 1960 a change was made in the standard for the meter.

The fault of any physical material standard for a linear measure is that its length remains fixed only under certain controlled conditions. The platinum standard meter bar would become longer than a meter if placed in an oven; or shorter than a meter if placed in a freezer. Science has devised a better way to determine length with extreme accuracy; a basis that is natural, uniform, and universal—the wavelength of light.

More than a century and a half after the scientists of the French Academy struggled so valiantly to determine a natural standard, the arbitrary standard that resulted has now been related to an unvarying natural one. A meter is now defined as 1,650,763.73 wavelengths of the orange-red radiation of krypton 86; or, putting it more scientifically, as 1,650,763.73 wavelengths in vacuum of the radiation corresponding to the transition between the levels $2p_{10}$ and $5d_5$ of the krypton 86 atom. Should all of the material standards for the meter be destroyed, any well-equipped physics laboratory can easily redetermine its length. However, the platinum-iridium bar standards are still important because of the ease with which they can be used for certain types of measurements.

By the turn of the twentieth century, 41 countries had adopted the metric system. In 26 it was the only official system and its use was compulsory; in the other 15 it was optional. During the present century the pace of acceptance accelerated. One hundred and twenty-seven countries, colonies, or protectorates have officially adopted the metric system or are in the throes of converting to it. Their people total over 90 percent of the world's population. In only 21 countries is the metric not the official system of weights and measures, although its use is legal in most of them.

The world's metric countries are:

Afghanistan

Albania

Algeria

Andorra

Angola

Argentina

Austria

Belgium

Bolivia

Brazil

Bulgaria

Burundi

Cambodia

Cameroon

Canary Islands

Cape Verde Islands

Central African Republic

Chad

Chile

China, People's Republic

Colombia

Congo

Congolese Republic

Costa Rica

Cuba

Czechoslovakia

Dahomey

Denmark

Dominican Republic

Ecuador

El Salvador

Equatorial Guinea

Ethiopia

Faroe Islands

Finland

France

French Guiana

French Somaliland

Gabon

German Democratic Republic

German Federal Republic
Greece
Greenland
Guadeloupe
Guatemala
Guinea
Haiti
Honduras
Hungary
Iceland
India
Indonesia
Iran
Iraq
Israel
Italy
Ivory Coast
Japan
Jordan
Korea, Republic
Laos
Lebanon
Libya
Liechtenstein
Luxemburg
Macao
Malagasy Republic
Mali
Martinique
Mauritania
Mauritius
Mexico
Monaco
Mongolia
Morocco
Mozambique
Nepal

Netherlands
Netherlands Antilles
New Caledonia
Nicaragua
Niger
Norway
Panama
Paraguay
Peru
Philippines
Poland
Portugal
Portuguese Guinea
Reunion
Rumania
Rwanda
San Marino
Sao Tome and Principe
Saudi Arabia
Senegal
Seychelles
Singapore
Somalia
Spain
Sudan
Surinam
Sweden
Switzerland
Syria
Taiwan
Thailand
Togo
Tunisia
Turkey
United Arab Republic
Upper Volta
Uruguay

U.S.S.R.                      Vietnam, Republic
Venezuela                     Yugoslavia


The following countries are in the process of converting to the metric system:

Eire                          South Africa
Ghana                         Tanzania
Kenya                         Uganda
Kuwait                        United Kingdom
Pakistan


The following countries do not use the metric system officially. In those bracketed it is used together with a local or the inch-pound system.

Australia                     Malawi
Barbados                      (Malaysia)
Botswana                      Malta
Burma                         (New Hebrides)
Canada                        New Zealand
Ceylon                        Sierra Leone
(Cyprus)                      Trinidad and Tobago
Gambia                        United States
Jamaica                       Western Samoa
Lesotho                       Zambia
Liberia


Well over half of the countries in which the metric system is not official are part of the British Commonwealth and, with the possible exception of Canada, they will probably follow England, whose target date for completing conversion is 1975. The nonmetric allies of the United States may soon be reduced to half a dozen political entities of the stature of Botswana, Lesotho, and Western Samoa.

Although more than nine out of ten people live in countries in which the metric is or soon will be the only system of weights and measures, all of them do not *use* it exclusively. In fact, there is no country in the world in which the pure metric system is used for all transactions in weights and measures. The most common variant is the continued use of old names for metric units. The best example of this is the pfund in Germany. Here the metric system has been the only legal system for about a century, but German housewives still buy meat and butter by the pfund, a name which has no place in the metric system. In old Prussia, a pfund used to equal 467.7 grams; throughout Germany the pfund now weighs 500 grams, one-half a kilogram. The difference of 33 grams is not very significant, but for 100 years the German people have insisted on calling one-half a kilogram a pound. In Spanish-speaking countries the use of the word quintal persists. This weight was originally 100 Spanish pounds. In some Latin American countries it is used to denote 100 kilograms; in others, 50 kilograms; in the Dominican Republic it equals 100 United States pounds.

In 1927, a Harvard professor made a survey of several European countries to determine the extent to which vestiges of premetric weights and measures persisted. Most of these countries had officially used the metric system exclusively for 50 to 100 or more years, yet Professor Kennelly found that

> . . . in any country that has adopted the metric system, there will always be vestiges of the original system or systems. It will be only a question of how many are left after a given period of time. Most of the old units gradually disappear; while others become metricised or modified in value to suit some convenient value in the metric system, and are then retained indefinitely.

In Belgium, which had been on the metric system for over 100 years, Professor Kennelly still found shops selling food by the livre of one-half a kilogram and the pinte of one-half a liter. In Holland, which had been metricized for a like period, cloth in remote areas was sometimes sold by the el of 70 centimeters and shop windows displayed prices by the pond and ons. The former equals 500 grams, the latter 100. In Italy practically all farmers measured grain by the staio (bushel), and in small towns food was sold by the libra (pound), in this case equal to a third of a kilogram. In Germany, many products were packaged or sold by the dutzend (dozen) or gross (12 dozen). Beer in Berlin was sold at wholesale by the tonne of 120 liters. The Rhineland inch of 26.5 millimeters was still a standard measurement in the lumber trade and carpentry.

Professor Kennelly found that it was possible to gauge the extent to which vestiges of old systems remained by studying school arithmetic books. In Spain, after more than 75 years in which the metric system was the only official system, school books still contained tables of conversion from the old system to the metric; in one book, the space devoted to a comparison of old and new measurements was double that devoted to the metric system.

The most surprising vestiges of old systems were found in France—surprising because the metric system had been born there more than a century and a quarter before the survey was made. All French roads are marked with signs giving distances in kilometers, but back in the hinterlands occasional road signs giving the distance to the next town in toises were still to be found. The Secretary of the French Academy of Agriculture summarized the situation by writing:

> In France, certain old measures are still occasionally applied in the country districts, always, of course, outside of official records. Some of them are correlated with the metric system, others are not. In the first category belong the toise of two meters, the pied of one-third meter, the boisseau of one-eighth and one-quarter hectoliters according to the district, the pinte of one-half liter, the livre of 500 grams, the arpent of one-half hectoliter. . . . In the second category belong the aune (ell) of 1.2 meters, the ligne of 0.00225 meter, the pouce of 0.027 meter . . . the tonneau of 1,000 liters . . . the acre, the verge, etc.

France is justly proud of the system of weights and measures that she created and, with minor exceptions, it is used exclusively throughout the country. But when 12 inches of snow falls and the weather bureau reports a depth of 305 millimeters, most Frenchmen still refer to a *pied de neige*. And in good French restaurants *escargots* are still served in units of a dozen rather than 10; the metal plates with 12 depressions for individual snails have never been changed, and it would not look well to leave two of them empty.

The continued use of nonmetric units after many decades is largely confined to the country districts. The application of old names to metric units, such as pfund, livre, pinte, etc., is more general. Another departure from the true metric system that is prevalent everywhere is the application of the binary number system to metric units. The equivalent of a pint of milk is called a half-liter, and of a half-pound of butter a quarter-kilo, although halves and quarters are not decimal expressions.

In most metric countries, nonmetric units continue to be used in some industries, sometimes side-by-side with metric units, sometimes independent of them. In general, this is true in industries that have a close association with the United States or Great Britain. For instance, the foundation of Japan's bicycle industry was in England and, although Japan is metricized, this industry continues to do business largely on an inch basis.

In countries that have been on the metric system for any length of time, all of these nonmetric instances are minor exceptions. Most people live by the metric system and young people know no other. The exceptions, which in every country have existed for many years after conversion, may be comforting to American and English housewives who fear that if the metric system is made official the pound and the quart will disappear from the supermarket shelves on a given day; or to motorists who are startled by the prospect of all road signs changing to kilometers overnight.

Since the establishment of the International Conference

on Weights and Measures—the body that controls the International Bureau—some changes have been made in the metric system, most of them of interest primarily to scientists and engineers. The change in the standard of the meter has already been mentioned. The standard of the second has been redefined to base it on an atomic rather than an astronomical constant. The second is now defined as the duration of 9,192,-631,770 cycles of the radiation associated with a specified transition of the cesium atom. This does not make any change in the second as a unit; it merely provides what is considered a more universal and accurate means of defining it.

The Conference has also added prefixes for both multiples and subdivisions to extend the scales of measurement. The prefix "tera" before meter or gram means one trillion, "giga" on billion, and "mega" one million. "Micro" means one-millionth, "nano" one-billionth, and "pico" one-trillionth. One of these prefixes has become familiar in the news in recent years; nuclear explosions are rated in megatons, the equivalent of 1,000,000 tons of TNT.

At its 1960 meeting, the International Convention—which meets every six years—reinterpreted the metric system in the *Système International d'Unites,* for which the abbreviation is S.I. in all languages. For all purposes other than scientific and advanced technical work, this is merely a change in name; actually it is a purification and extension of the metric system to make it truly universal. Through the years, several systems had developed that were all metric but which differed in detail in various parts of the world and among members of different professions. For instance, some scientists used the gram, the centimeter, and the second as basic units under a system called "g.c.s." Others used the meter, the kilogram, and the second (m.k.s.). Both are metric systems, but only the latter is part of the S.I.

The S.I. also formalized the extension of the metric system to six basic units. Long ago, the second was adopted as the unit of time in both the g.c.s. and m.k.s. applications of the system. To link mechanical units to electromagnetic units, the ampere, the unit of electric current, was added in 1935, making four basic units. In 1954, two other units were added: the candela, the unit of light, and the Kelvin, the unit of temperature.

The Kelvin scale of temperature starts at absolute zero—the temperature at which molecular activity ceases. It has a fixed point of 273.16 kelvins at the triple point of water—the temperature at which water can exist in three states: solid, liquid, and gas. This is very slightly above what is commonly called the freezing point. In metric countries, the Kelvin scale is used only for scientific work; for other purposes temperature is recorded by the Celsius scale. Americans call this centigrade, but the International Bureau has renamed it Celsius after the Swedish astronomer who invented it. Zero in the Celsius scale is the freezing point of water at a certain pressure. The two systems compare with the Fahrenheit system as follows:

|  | KELVIN | CELSIUS | FAHRENHEIT |
|---|---|---|---|
| Absolute zero | 0 | −273.15 | −459.67 |
| Water freezes | 273.15 | 0 | 32 |
| Body temperature | 310.15 | 37 | 98.6 |
| Water boils | 373.15 | 100 | 212 |

The basic units of the complete S.I. system, of which what was formerly the metric system is now a part, are:

| Length | —meter (m) |
|---|---|
| Mass | —kilogram (kg) |
| Time | —second (s) |
| Electric Current | —ampere (A) |
| Temperature | —kelvin (K) |
| Luminous Intensity | —candela (cd) |

(Exact definitions of the basic units of the S.I. system, a complete list of multiples and subdivisions, lists of derived units and supplementary units with their abbreviations, and approximate and exact relationships of common metric units to Customary units will be found in the appendix.)

In addition to its basic units, the S.I. system includes a number of derived units for the measurement of, among others, force, energy, and power. Under the Customary System, mass and force may be expressed in the same unit—for instance, both in pounds. This is unsatisfactory for scientific work because the relationship between mass and gravitational force varies under different conditions. Under the S.I. system, only mass—and never force—is measured by kilograms. The unit of force is the "newton" (N), one of which is defined as the amount of force that, acting for one second on one kilogram of matter, will increase its speed by one meter per second. The newton is named for the famous English formulator of the laws of mechanics who, according to legend, "discovered" gravity by being hit on the head by a falling apple while sitting under a tree. Appropriately, one newton is just about the gravitational force of an average falling apple.

Energy has many forms: the kinetic energy of motion, the potential energy of the coiled spring, thermal energy, electrical energy. But all energy is basically the product of force and distance, and is convertible from one form to another. Hence, the S.I. system uses one unit for all kinds of energy—the "joule" (J), which is the amount of energy needed to push a distance of one meter against a force of one newton.

When Watt perfected the steam engine it replaced the horse and it was natural for customers to want to know its capability in terms of the horse, so steam engines and, later, internal combustion engines were rated in horsepower. When the electric motor arrived its unit of power was named after Watt. No matter what form power takes it is a rate of generation or dissipation of energy, so the only unit of power in the S.I. system is called the watt (W), which represents one joule of energy per second. One horsepower is equal to

745.6988 watts, which electrical engineers have rounded off to 746 watts.

The derived units, as well as the ampere, the kelvin, and the candela, are important to scientists and engineers but of only academic interest to most people, whose concern with weights and measures is largely restricted to units of length, weight, and capacity. The most commonly used metric units of length in everyday life are the millimeter (mm) for small dimensions, the centimeter (cm) for daily practical use, the meter (m) for expressing dimensions of larger objects and short distances, and the kilometer (km) for longer distances. There are approximately 25 millimeters to the inch (exactly 25.4). The centimeter is about four-tenths of an inch (3.95+). The meter is slightly less than 40 inches (39.62+ inches), and the kilometer about six-tenths of a mile (0.62+ mile). The metric system has no basic unit equivalent to the English foot; most metric countries use a 30-centimeter measuring stick, which is only about two-tenths of an inch less than a foot.

Small areas are usually expressed in square centimeters (cm²), larger ones by the square meter (m²), which is about 20 percent larger than a square yard. The hectare (ha), which has been used for land surveys but is not recognized in the S.I. system, is slightly less than 2½ acres (2.47+ acres).

The most convenient unit of volume for everyday use is the liter (l), although it is part of the S.I. system only to the extent that it is recognized as a special name for the cubic decimeter that may be used for nonscientific work. There is no international standard liter. For many years, the liter was considered as being a volume of water equal to a platinum-iridium kilogram standard at the International Standards Organization. Some years ago it was found that, due to changes in the temperature and pressure at which water was weighed, the kilogram standard actually equalled 1.000028 dm³ instead of 1 dm³. A difference of 28 hundred-thousandths does not affect the measurement of milk or gasoline, but it makes the liter a second-class citizen among units for precise work.

One liter is very slightly larger than the United States liquid quart (1.05+ quarts). For cooking recipes, small quantities are usually expressed in milliliters (ml). Precise measurements of volume in science and pharmacy are expressed in cubic centimeters (cm³) or cubic millimeters (mm³). For measurements of large volume, as in excavations or poured concrete, the cubic meter (m³) is used; it is about 30 percent greater than a cubic yard.

The most common unit of mass or weight is the kilogram (kg), which equals about 2.2 pounds (2.20+). For other than binary divisions of the kilogram the gram (g) is used; there are approximately 28 grams to the avoirdupois ounce (0.035 ounce). Scientists and pharmacists use subdivisions of the gram. The metric ton (t) is 1,000 kilograms (2,204.6 pounds), almost equal to the British long ton and about 10 percent more than the American short ton.

There are alternate ways of expressing most measures under the metric system. Three-quarters of a meter might be expressed as 7 decimeters, 50 millimeters. More commonly it would be 750 millimeters. One and one-third meters might be 1 meter, 3 decimeters, 33 millimeters; 1,333 millimeters; or, more commonly, 1.333 meters.

There is continuing interest among metrologists in redefining standards in terms of natural constants, as the meter and the second have already been redefined. The kilogram is the only basic unit that is still represented by a material standard. Although some proposals have been made for possible atomic standards of mass, an early change in this area does not seem likely.

There is some talk of decimalizing time and angles; 60 seconds and 360° are difficult units to work with. One scientist has recently proposed the extension of the metric system in these areas by using a 20-hour day and a 200° circle. The latter would be based on a "decimal degree," one-hundredth of the angle we now call 180°. Thus a right angle would be 50°, the sum of the angle in a triangle would be 100°, a circle and the sum of the internal angles of a quadrangle would be

200°. From this, it would be an easy step to a fundamental decimal unit of time, the "decimal hour" being the length of time required for the earth to rotate through 10 decimal degrees. This would give 20 hours in the day—10 hours of daylight and 10 hours of night at the equinox. The hour would be divided decimally; there would be no minutes and seconds as such. What is now 6:30 P.M. would be 5.5 hours— two seconds later the time would be 5.52 hours.

The author of this system points to the benefits it will bring to calculations involving time and angles, both in shortening the process by bringing them fully under the decimal system and in avoiding possible error. It would be particularly beneficial in astronavigation and the launching of satellites. He admits that it would be "extremely costly, but it might be justified on the premise that mankind is now only at the dawn of its development. Recorded history goes back only about 5,000 years and astronomers say that we can probably count on the earth's remaining habitable for over a billion more years."

Such a radical change is not being currently considered as a development of the S.I. system; the second will probably remain, defined in atomic terms, as the unit of time. The next major development will probably be the addition of a unit to measure sound, which is currently lacking in the S.I. system.

# 4

# THE SYSTEMS COMPARED

For almost 200 years, every American who visited England commented on the absurdity of British currency before its conversion to a decimal system. How, they asked, could any people live with a currency that involved dividing by 12 and 20 to find out how much money they had spent? If one bought several items and wanted to determine the total cost, it was necessary to add the pennies, divide by 12, and carry over to the shillings column; add the shillings, divide by 20, and carry over to the pounds column; then add the pounds. How ridiculous and complex was this compared to merely adding dollars and cents.

Few American visitors commented on the absurdity of the Imperial system of weights and measures. They were used to the same system at home and did not consider it ridiculous to add inches and divide by 12 to get feet or add ounces and divide by 16 to get pounds or 32 (40 in England) to get quarts. They had done it all their lives; it was the American system and they were proud of it. When they went to France they were confused by measurements in meters, liters, and kilos and damned this as a complicated foreign system which only the devious French could live with.

Surely a visitor to the United States from another planet would marvel at the inconsistency of a people who have a simple, logical system of currency but still measure things by using three different numerical systems that involve mixed numbers, fractions, and such complex concepts as lowest common denominators; and apply this mixture to scores of unrelated units of measurements derived from such standards as the length of three barleycorns and the girth of an Anglo-Saxon monarch. The objective observer would find it particularly hard to understand why Americans continue to do this when virtually all other people on the planet use a system of weights and measures similar in its most important aspect to American currency. His confusion would be complete when he was told that the United States was the first nation to adopt a decimal currency.

One reason that Americans supinely accept their illogical system of weights and measures is that they do not know that a better system exists. This may seem surprising in an age of universal education, but it was confirmed by a recent Gallup poll in which people were asked the question, "Do you know what the metric system is?" Over 9 out of 10 grade school graduates (93 percent) replied in the negative; almost 3 out of 4 (71 percent) high school graduates said No. Only among college graduates did a majority of the respondents—67 percent—answer in the affirmative. It seems incomprehensible that anybody could spend 4 years in college without learning what the metric system is, but one person out of 3 was apparently able to do it. And it must be assumed that many of those polled who said that they knew what the metric system is merely knew its name without knowing how it worked. If this poll is accurate, it is safe to say that a *very* large majority of Americans do not know anything about the metric system. They may have heard some humorous allusions to the system which do not help to give an impression of its simplicity: "I Love You a Hectoliter and a Decaliter," or "I wouldn't touch it with a 3.048-meter pole."

This same Gallup poll also asked, "Would you like to see the U.S. adopt the metric system?" A majority of affirmative answers came only from college graduates; 55 percent said

Yes, 30 percent said No, and 15 percent had no opinion. More than half of those with lesser education were against a change. High school graduates replied 25 percent yes, 58 percent no, and 17 percent no opinion; among grade school graduates the percentages were 20, 56, and 24. It is an interesting commentary on one aspect of human nature—the desire to retain that which is familiar regardless of its merits—that although 9 out of 10 of the least educated group said that they did not know what the metric system is, over half of them did not want to use it.

At first glance, the complete metric system may look complicated to someone who has no previous knowledge of it. He sees long lists of multisyllabic foreign words, 13 of them to define linear units alone, and equally extensive lists for units of mass and capacity. Words like terameter, gigameter, manometer, and picometer are frightening. And if the initiate is then presented with a list of derived units he is introduced to joule, hertz, newton, and several other incomprehensible terms. The need to learn all this would seem to be a good reason for not adopting the metric system; although the complete system, including all the derived units and all multiples and subdivisions of the basic units, involves fewer terms than the complete Customary System.

Actually, it is not necessary to learn the complete metric system in order to use it in everyday life, any more than it is necessary to know the complete Customary System. Those who are not engaged in scientific or technical work can go through life quite happily with the meter, centimeter, millimeter, and kilometer for length; the gram and kilogram for weight; and the liter and milliliter for capacity. These 8 units replace the equivalent 14 common units that one must know to use the Customary System. In everyday practice, the prefixes deca (or deka), deci, and hecto are seldom used in metric countries; a tenth of a liter is usually called 100ml rather than a decaliter, a hectometer is usually called 100m.

To know the commonly used units in the metric system it is necessary to memorize only the following:

```
    10 millimeters (mm) = 1 centimeter (c)
 1,000 millimeters      = 1 meter (m)
   100 centimeters      = 1 meter
 1,000 meters           = 1 kilometer (km)
 1,000 grams (g)        = 1 kilogram(kg)
 1,000 kilograms        = 1 metric ton (t)
 1,000 milliliters      = 1 liter (l)
```

The only numbers involved in the relation of the common metric units are 10, 100, and 1,000. Contrast this with the 29 numbers—many of them multi-digit—with which a child must clutter his memory to really learn the relationship of the most commonly used units of the Customary System, not including such things as rods, fathoms, furlongs, and troy weight.

### Linear units:

```
    12 in. = 1 ft.
     3 ft. = 1 yd.
    36 in. = 1 yd.
 1,760 yds. = 1 mi.
 5,280 ft. = 1 mi.
```

### Units of area:

```
         9 sq. ft.  = 1 sq. yd.
       144 sq. in.  = 1 sq. ft.
     1,296 sq. in.  = 1 sq. yd.
 3,097,600 sq. yds. = 1 sq. mi.
27,878,400 sq. ft.  = 1 sq. mi.
       640 acres    = 1 sq. mi.
     4,840 sq yds.  = 1 acre
    43,560 sq. ft.  = 1 acre
```

### Units of weight:

```
    16 oz.  = 1 lb.
 2,000 lbs. = 1 ton
```

### Units of quantity:

```
    12 = 1 doz.
   144 = 1 gross
```

Units of liquid measure:

| | | | |
|---|---|---|---|
| $\underline{16}$ | ozs. | = | 1 pt. |
| $\underline{32}$ | ozs. | = | 1 qt. |
| $\underline{2}$ | pts. | = | 1 qt. |
| $\underline{4}$ | qts. | = | 1 gal. |
| $\underline{8}$ | pts. | = | 1 gal. |
| $\underline{128}$ | ozs. | = | 1 gal. |
| $\underline{231}$ | cu. in. | = | 1 gal. |

Units of dry measure:

| | | | |
|---|---|---|---|
| $\underline{8}$ | qts. | = | 1 peck |
| $\underline{32}$ | qts. | = | 1 bu. |
| $\underline{4}$ | pecks | = | 1 bu. |
| $\underline{2,150.42}$ | cu. in. | = | 1 bu. |

(That is, a struck bushel;
a heaped bushel is
$\underline{2,747.715}$ cu. in.)

If the child does not remember all of these numbers he can determine them by computation—if he knows the formulae. Three squared or three cubed are simple computations to determine the number of feet in a square and cubic yard. Computing square feet in a square mile—multiplying 5,280 by 5,280—takes somewhat longer. And if the student is asked to compute the number of acres in a square mile he must first know the number of feet in a mile and the number of square feet in an acre. Then he must work out $\frac{5,280^2}{43,560}$, which takes quite a bit of time and a lot of paper—and the lengthy calculation offers considerable opportunity for error.

It is reasonably safe to say that nobody except those who use them in their work remembers all of the numbers that are necessary to relate the common units of the Customary System. Beyond such basics as 3 feet to the yard and 16 ounces to the pound, most people would have to use a reference book to determine relationships. Yet everybody learned these numbers in school, spending many boring hours to acquire knowledge that was promptly forgotten.

In the metric system, computations merely involve moving a decimal point; multiplying or dividing by 10, 100, or 1,000. If a child is asked how many square millimeters there are in a square centimeter he converts a centimeter to ten millimeters by moving the decimal point one place to the right and then multiplies 10mm by 10mm by moving it another place to the right to get 100mm. If a metric student is asked how many hectares make a square kilometer he must first know that a hectare is 10,000m². A square kilometer is 1,000m × 1,000m. To multiply, he moves the decimal point 3 places to the right and gets 1,000,000m². To divide 1,000,000 by 10,000 he moves the decimal point 4 places to the left and arrives at 10 hectares to a square kilometer.

A graphic comparison is shown on the chart on page 64.

Because so much emphasis must be placed on fractions in schools to equip students to use the Customary System many Americans find decimal arithmetic involving four or more digits confusing. Foreign children are so much at home in the system that they can convert units mentally. To multiply in the decimal system the point is moved to the right by one place less than there are digits in the multiplier; 10,000 × 100 = 1,000,000. To divide, the decimal point is moved to the left one place less than there are digits in the divisor: 10,000 ÷ 100 = 100.

Metric opponents claim that the nomenclature of the Customary System is much simpler because it is limited to easy, one-syllable words. To use the common units of this system a child must learn fifteen words: inch, foot, yard, mile, acre, ounce, pound, ton, pint, quart, gallon, peck, bushel, dozen, and gross—and remember that there are two different ounces and quarts. To use the equivalent units in the metric system a child need learn only eight words, seven of them of one syllable. Meter, liter, and gram combined with the prefixes milli-, centi-, and kilo- cover all the common units except the hectare and the metric ton.

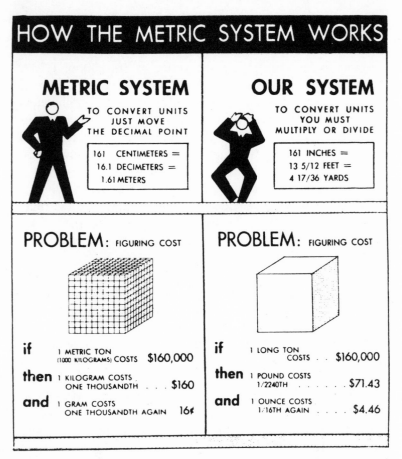

# HOW THE METRIC SYSTEM WORKS

## METRIC SYSTEM

TO CONVERT UNITS
JUST MOVE
THE DECIMAL POINT

161 CENTIMETERS =
16.1 DECIMETERS =
1.61 METERS

## OUR SYSTEM

TO CONVERT UNITS
YOU MUST
MULTIPLY OR DIVIDE

161 INCHES =
13 5/12 FEET =
4 17/36 YARDS

**PROBLEM:** FIGURING COST

**if** 1 METRIC TON
(1000 KILOGRAMS) COSTS $160,000

**then** 1 KILOGRAM COSTS
ONE THOUSANDTH . . . $160

**and** 1 GRAM COSTS
ONE THOUSANDTH AGAIN 16¢

**PROBLEM:** FIGURING COST

**if** 1 LONG TON
COSTS . . $160,000

**then** 1 POUND COSTS
1/2240TH . . . . . . $71.43

**and** 1 OUNCE COSTS
1/16TH AGAIN . . . . $4.46

from Twentieth Yearbook of the National Council of Teachers of
Mathematics, published by Bureau of Publications, Teachers College,
Columbia University. Copyright 1948.

Even the names for the derived units in the S.I. system may
be easier to learn if one remembers that most are named after
men who had something to do with the discovery of the principles involved. Newton was an English mathematician, Joule
and Kelvin were English physicists, and Watt was a Scottish
engineer. Other units are named for Ampère, a French physicist (electric current), Henry, an American physicist (induc-
tance), Volta, an Italian physicist (volt-electrical potential),

Faraday, an English physicist (farad-electric capacitance), Ohm, a German physicist (electric resistance), Weber, a German physicist (magnetic flux), Hertz, a German physicist (frequency), and Pascal, a French mathematician (pressure).

To compare the metric and Customary systems properly it is necessary to consider both in terms of how different groups of people use weights and measures. Obviously, an engineer or a physicist is more involved with measurements than a secretary or a truck driver. For purposes of comparison, the total population may be divided into five groups: 1. the general public, 2. people who use numbers or measurements in their work, 3. engineers, 4. scientists, and 5. students.

For common use by all people both systems are about equally satisfactory *after they have been learned*. The metric system is much easier to learn, and that is an advantage for students. The principal use of weights and measures by most people in their daily lives does not involve calculations. They are concerned only with how big something is, or how long, or how much it contains or weighs. For ordinary measurements, where no calculations are involved, the handier system is that with which an individual is familiar. It is just as easy to buy milk by the quart as by the liter, to measure a board in inches or in centimeters, or to buy 5 pounds of potatoes or 2½ kilos. It is ridiculous to say, as many metric opponents do, that the units of the Customary System are "handier." They are handier only to those who know them. To one who knows only the metric system, nothing could be more unhandy than a 12-inch foot or a 16-ounce pound.

If we were to change to the metric system, it would make little difference in everyday measurements after one learned the units. A 132-pound woman might be thrilled that she suddenly weighed 60 (in kilos), and a potential Miss America would be proud of her 91 bust (in centimeters). However, women who wear a size 14 dress might be distressed at changing to a size 40. Admittedly, it would take some time for sports fans to get used to the Indiana 800, a touchdown from the 3m line, or a 155m home run. But hot-rodders would be happy with a car that accelerated to 84 km per hour in 10 seconds; it sounds faster than 69 mph. A pound of butter would be replaced by a half-kilo, about 10 percent more. Milk would be sold by the liter, about 5 percent more. The equivalent of a fifth of whiskey would be a four-fifths of whiskey, also about 5 percent more. A place that was 20 miles away would be 32 km distant, a ratio of 1 to 1.6.

As soon as calculations enter the picture the advantage of the metric system becomes apparent. This is true no matter how simple or complex the calculation. For an American housewife to determine how many 4-oz. portions there are in a can containing 1 lb. 7 oz. she must first convert the weight to 23 oz. and then divide by 4. To get the number of 120g portions in a 700g can the French housewife merely divides 70 by 12. It is much easier to compare prices under the metric system. If an American housewife wants to make a rough comparison between a "large" size box containing 1 lb. 7 oz. selling for 59¢ and a "giant economy" size containing 2 lb. 3 oz. selling for 79¢ she must first transpose both to ounces and then divide 59¢ by 23 ozs. and 79¢ by 35 ozs. to learn that the giant economy size is a fake bargain. A French housewife comparing the prices of a 700g box at 59¢ and a 1050g box at 88¢ merely has to divide 59¢ by 7 and 88¢ by 10+ to get the relative cost per 100g and learn that the smaller box is the better buy.

The United States has laws governing the labeling of the weight or capacity of packages, but a common practice in merchandising packaged goods is to make the unit seem bigger by package design or misleading labeling that is within the law. Many products are packaged in "nonsense" quantities; 6¼ ounces to stimulate a half-pound or 19¾ ounces to simulate a pound and a half. A giant box of detergent may be labeled 368 ounces. The buyer cannot compare units so labeled or even determine what is in them without dividing by 16.

An instance of misleading labeling is a bottle of barbecue sauce, packaged by a leading food company, that has a label around the neck proclaiming in letters almost a half-inch high, "18 ozs." Since barbecue sauce is a liquid and liquids are usually measured in liquid ounces the natural assumption is that the bottle contains something over a pint. If the buyer reads the small print on the bottom of the main label she finds that the 18 ounces refers to weight, not capacity. Eighteen avoirdupois ounces of a liquid with this specific gravity equals slightly *less* than 16 fluid ounces. Such misleading labeling is impossible under the metric system. In a metric country, the contents of the bottle would be given in either milliliters or grams; there would be no possibility of confusion.

Computations of length are much simpler in millimeters than in feet, inches, and fractions of inches. Consider a man using the Customary System who wants to figure the amount of lumber required to build something which has units of 2′ 10½″, 7′ 7 13/16″, 5′ 6″, and 3′ 9⅝″. First he must reduce all of his fractional inches to sixteenths and then perform this calculation:

| 2 ft. | 10 in. | 8 sixteenths |
| 7 ft. | 7 in. | 13 sixteenths |
| 5 ft. | 6 in. | |
| 3 ft. | 9 in. | 10 sixteenths |
| 17 ft. | 32 in. | 31 sixteenths |

He then divides 31 by 16 and carries over to the inch column and 33 by 12 and carries over to the foot column to find out that he needs 19′ 9 15/16″ of lumber.

Contrast this with the man who is building the same thing working in the metric system with dimensions expressed in millimeters. He merely adds a column of figures and moves a decimal point, thus:

876mm
2,332mm
1,676mm
1,159mm
6,043mm or 6.043m of lumber

In calculations of area, the arithmetic required by the Customary System is still more extensive in relation to that of the metric. Consider a man who wants to determine how much seed he needs to plant a lawn 35′ 5″ by 26′ 4″ if one pound of seed covers 75 sq. ft.

$$35′ \ 5″ \ = \ 425″$$
$$26′ \ 4″ \ = \ 316″$$
$$425″ \times 316″ \ = \ 134,200 \ \text{sq. in.}$$
$$134,200 \ \div \ 144 \ = \ 932+ \ \text{sq. ft.}$$
$$932 \ \div \ 75 \ = \ \text{approximately } 12\frac{1}{2} \ \text{lbs.}$$

(Or this could be done by changing the inches to decimal equivalents of a foot by multiplying .0833 by five and four respectively to get 35.516′ × 29.333′ and then multiplying these to get the area. Either method is about equally lengthy.)

The same lawn in France would measure 10.80m by 8.05m and an equal density of seed would be about 1 kg per 15m$^2$:

$$10.80\text{m} \times 8.05\text{m} \ = \ 86.94$$
$$86.94 \ \div \ 15 \ = \ \text{approximately } 5.8 \ \text{kg}$$

If a woman wants to determine what carpet for her living room will cost she has to go through the same type of computation because rooms are normally measured in feet and carpet is sold by the square yard—or if she measures her room in yards she comes out with fractions that have to be multiplied.

The greater simplicity of the metric system is most apparent in determining capacity of a cubical or rectangular container or the weight of its contents. A simple problem of this type is worked out in detail in two columns below to dramatize the difference in the calculation involved.

*Customary System*

Given a cubical tank 6′9½″ each way, filled with water: find
(1) the volume in cubic feet,
(2) volume in gallons,
(3) weight of water in pounds.

1. Convert 6′9½″ to inches:

$$\begin{array}{r} 12 \\ \times 6 \\ \hline 72 \\ 9\frac{1}{2} \\ \hline 81\frac{1}{2} \text{ or } 81.5 \end{array}$$

2. Multiply length by width by height.

$$\begin{array}{r} 81.5 \\ 81.5 \\ \hline 4075 \\ 815 \\ 6520 \\ \hline 6642.25 \\ 81.5 \\ \hline 3321125 \\ 664225 \\ 5313800 \\ \hline 541343.375 \text{ cubic inches} \end{array}$$

3. Remembering that there are 1,728 cubic inches in a cubic foot, divide by 1,728.

*Metric System*

Given a cubical tank 2.07 meters each way, filled with water: find
(1) the volume in cubic meters,
(2) volume in liters,
(3) weight of water in kilograms.

1. Multiply length by width by height.

$$\begin{array}{r} 2.07 \\ 2.07 \\ \hline 1449 \\ 414 \\ \hline 4.2849 \\ 2.07 \\ \hline 299943 \\ 85698 \\ \hline 8.869743 \text{ cubic meters} \end{array}$$

2. As there are 1,000 liters in a cubic meter the number of liters in the tank is determined by moving the decimal point three places to the right—8,869.743 liters.

3. A liter of water weighs one kilogram; so, the water weighs 8,869.743 kilograms.

```
              313.277+ cu. ft.
1728 ) 541343.375
       5184
       2294
       1728
       5663
       5184
       4793
       3456
      13377
      12096
      12815
      12096
        719
```

4. Remembering that there are 231 cubic inches in a gallon, divide this into the number of cubic inches in the tank.

```
         2343.477+  gallons
231 ) 541343.375
      462
      793
      693
     1004
      924
      803
      693
     1103
      924
     1797
     1617
     1805
     1617
      188
```

5. Remembering that a cubic
foot of water weighs 62½
pounds, multiply the number
of cubic feet in the tank by
62.5.

$$313.277 \; + \; \text{cubic feet}$$
$$62.5$$
$$\overline{1566385}$$
$$626554$$
$$1879662$$
$$\overline{19579.8125} \; \text{pounds}$$

Under the metric system, the problem involves 39 digits, and multiplication and division is done by moving a decimal point. Under the Customary System the problem involves 249 digits in 5 lengthy steps of multiplication and division, with the consequent possibility of error. Furthermore, the answer under the Customary System is only approximate; there is an inaccuracy of about 11 pounds due to dropping the clumsy fraction. And this is a relatively easy problem; it would be much more complex if the tank was rectangular with dimensions such as 3′7⅛″ × 1′2¾″ × 4′9 5/16″.

In testifying before a Senate committee considering a bill to adopt the metric system, Alexander Graham Bell illustrated the ease of determining capacity and weight from metric linear dimensions even in very large numbers by citing a hypothetical tank containing 123,456,789 cubic units of water of which he wanted to know the weight and volume. He said:

> I will not attempt to work the result out to its final conclusion [using the Customary System] even with the aid of paper and pencil, for I must confess that my memory does not hold the exact number of cubic inches contained in a gallon and I have no means of recovering this knowledge excepting by reference to a printed table. Then again my memory does not retain a distinct impression of the relation of weight to volume of water on our present system. The

problem is therefore absolutely insoluble to me at the present moment. I must consult some reference book for the information that would enable me to work it out. But put the problem in metrical terms and the problem is solved as soon as you have ascertained the cubical contents in any of the metrical denominations you prefer; the translation of the result into other more convenient denominations of the metrical system requires no calculation and is a mere question of putting the decimal point in the proper place. For example, suppose we find that our tank holds 123,456,789 cubic centimeters of water. How many liters have we there, and how much does the water weigh? The answer is 123,456.789 liters weighing 123,456.789 kilograms.

But, says the metric opponent, such problems are of concern only to school children or engineers; how many times in practice does one have to compute cubic capacity or determine the weight of water?

It is conceivable that a man who wants to build a stand to hold a large aquarium would have to know how much the aquarium weighed when full, or that a person building a bin for feed or fertilizer would have to know how big it should be to hold a certain amount or how much a bin of a given size would hold. And if one wants to buy an air conditioner the first question that the salesman asks is, "What is the cubic content of the area?" In short, a system of weights and measures is not very sensible if most people cannot apply it without recourse to reference books, or if its application involves lengthy mathematical calculations.

Those who minimize the importance of the uniform relationship of metric units of length, weight, and capacity point out that these relationships are based on the weight on volume of water and do not apply to anything else. Alexander Graham Bell gave this demonstration to show the ease with which conversions could be made to other substances.

There is a simple relation between volume and weight: one cubic centimeter of water weighs one gram. The fact remembered is the key to the whole subject. Now if you want to calculate the weight of any other substance you have simply to express its volume in cubic centimeters and multiply that by the specific gravity of the substance. Here is a piece of steel 10 centimeters long, one centimeter wide, and one-tenth of a centimeter thick (one millimeter). What is its weight?

Now you first find out the cubical contents of this piece of steel by multiplying together the length, breadth, and thickness expressed in centimeters so as to have the answer in cubic centimeters. It is 10 centimeters long and 1 centimeter wide; 10 times 1 is 10. It has a surface of 10 square centimeters, it is one-tenth of a centimeter thick. One-tenth of 10 is 1; that is, its volume is 1 cubic centimeter. Now multiply this by the specific gravity of steel and this will give you its weight expressed in grams. The specific gravity of steel, if I remember rightly, is somewhere about 8; that is, a piece of steel weighs about 8 times its own volume of water. Eight times 1 is 8. This piece of steel then weighs about 8 grams.

The same principle that applies to the general public applies to those people who use numbers or measurements in their work; so long as they are concerned only with measurements there is little difference between the systems; when calculations are involved the simplicity of the metric system is apparent. There is no difference in the use of metric and inch measuring tools. The operation of a micrometer is the same whether it is calibrated in decimal inches or divisions of millimeters. Some who oppose the metric system in this a ea claim that micrometers calibrated in hundredths of a millimeter (1/2,500″ approximately) are too fine while those calibrated in tenths of a millimeter (1/250″ approximately) are not fine enough. In practice most metric micrometers are calibrated in .05mm (2/1,000″ approximately).

The inherent advantage of the decimal basis of the metric system is evidenced by the fact that, in several fields, linear measurements are made by decimalizing customary units. Machining of metal is done in terms of thousandths of an inch.

Surveyors are stuck with the 5,280′ mile but they decimalize the foot. An engineer's chain is 100 feet with the foot decimalized.

Calculations in the construction industry are far easier in the metric system because many of them involve computation of area or volume. Figuring the amount and cost of lumber needed for siding or cement for a foundation involves the same methods in each system as figuring the seed for a lawn or the volume of a cube. In several areas of retailing, inventories are simpler under the metric system. Hardware dealers or haberdashers, for instance, buy many things by the dozen or gross and sell them by the unit. Wrote one, "What a nuisance it always is to divide the invoiced price by twelve and at inventory time to reverse the process by counting the packages and then multiplying by twelve on so many, many items."

Consider the poor pharmacist. To measure by the scruple, which is unique to his trade, he has to know all this:

| | | |
|---|---|---|
| 0.05 | apothecaries' scruple | = 1 grain |
| 0.15432356 | apothecaries' scruple | = 1 carat |
| 1.2 | apothecaries' scruples | = 1 troy pennyweight |
| 1.367187 | apothecaries' scruples | = 1 avoirdupois dram |
| 3. | apothecaries' scruples | = 1 apothecaries' dram |
| 21.875 | apothecaries' scruples | = 1 avoirdupois ounce |
| 24. | apothecaries' scruples | = 1 apothecaries' ounce |
| 288. | apothecaries' scruples | = 1 apothecaries' pound |
| 350. | apothecaries' scruples | = 1 avoirdupois pound |

Today's druggists are thankful that the scruple and other special units of apothecary measure are going into oblivion. Medical schools started to teach students to write prescriptions in metric units years ago and almost all prescriptions are so written today. When the few aged doctors who still use the old system die off or retire druggists may bury the scruple. Until the metric system became universal in the pharmaceutical industry retail druggists bought domestically packaged drugs by avoirdupois weight and dispensed them by troy weight; the pound that he bought contained 16 ounces of 437.5 grains but the pound that he sold contained 12 ounces of 480 grains.

The metric system is particularly advantageous in medicine and pharmacy because accuracy is so vitally important. There is much less chance of error if the metric system is used in every step from the research department of the pharmaceutical company to the retail druggist compounding a prescription. Prescriptions are easier to write and interpret in the whole numbers of the metric system. Dosages that are governed by body weight can be more exact when both the drug and the weight are expressed in the same units. Also, a doctor can obtain a better appreciation of the distribution of drugs throughout the system through metric reports on concentrations of the drug in the urine and blood.

One advantage of the universal use of the metric system for many business transactions and much record keeping is in the smaller number of units and the elimination of the need for conversion when material is originally measured by another system. For instance, the Office of Emergency Planning published a listing of stockpile objectives for many strategic materials which includes weights in troy ounces, avoirdupois ounces, pounds, short tons, and long tons. Many of these commodities are imported; so, to compile the list, O.E.P. has to convert from grams, kilograms, and metric tons.

Engineers will be more affected by a change to the metric system than any other group—except children in schools—for no other profession is more intimately associated with precise measurements and computations based on measurements. It has been estimated that the exclusive use of S.I. units in engineering computations shortens them by some 60 percent to 80 percent in length and time. Modern technology increasingly demands a closer relationship between scientists and engineers. The adoption of the metric system in engineering would improve communications with the scientists who already use it. In fact, it would make communication easier between research, design, and development engineers, who use metric units, and production engineers, who still work in the inch-pound system.

Electrical engineers and chemical engineers already use metric units extensively. Many of the derived units in the S.I. system have long been universally used in electrical work throughout the world—even the American consumer buys his electricity by kilowatt-hours. Most American engineers in other fields—construction, mining, manufacturing—have been trained in the Customary System and cling to it tenaciously because it is the system that they know.

A mining engineer who worked long enough in metric countries to become familiar with the system wrote this criticism of the American way:

> All mining operations involve moving a certain *weight* and *volume* a certain *distance* horizontally and vertically. The fact that there is no relationship between volume and weight and distance only adds to the arithmetic that the engineer must do and multiplies the possibility of error. When we consider the details, such as pumping out the water which seeps through the earth, we have to dodge back and forth from cubic feet to gallons, to pounds, to feet (of lift), to square inches (the cross section of the pipe), to cubic inches (the cross section area multiplied by the stroke of the pumps). . . . To pump away an acre-foot of water, we say: 7½ gallons to the cubic foot, for 43,560 cubic feet, amounts to 326,700 gallons. (Actually it is not 7½ gallons to the cubic foot, but 7.4805, which makes a difference of about 1,000 gallons.) If we require the *weight* of that much water, we have first to multiply to get pounds and then to divide to get tons.
>
> A hectare, on the contrary, measures 100 meters by 100 meters, an area of 10,000 square meters. A water source with an area of 1 hectare which was 1 meter deep would therefore contain 10,000 cubic meters; that is to say, it would hold water amounting to 10,000 tons, if we would know its weight, and 10,000,000 liters, if we are dealing with quantity. . . . Calculating a water supply in acre-feet and the

consumption of that water in gallons per capita per diem ought to bring us right up short: *Look here, are we deliberately trying to do this the hard way?*

The simplicity and uniformity of the derived S.I. units make engineering calculations far easier. Under the American system, engineers must take into consideration such conversions as 1 hp. = 550 ft. lbs., or 1 British thermal unit (B.T.U.) = 778 ft. lbs. and multiply by these odd figures in their calculations to determine power or fuel consumption. Also American engineers and technicians who do not know the metric system are handicapped by their inability to comprehend material in foreign journals and papers. Abstracts of important foreign literature are available in translation in engineering libraries but usually the metric units in which they were written are not converted.

In engineering, international communication would be helpful; in science, it is essential. Scientific progress would be greatly retarded without a common language of measurements in which scientists throughout the world can express their theories and findings. Because of its greater simplicity, exactness, and accuracy, the metric system became that language many years ago and is now universally used in almost every science. Scientists who work in metrics have long advocated its general adoption in the United States. Their principal association is on record to this effect: "*Resolved*, that the American Association for the Advancement of Science reaffirms its belief in the desirability of the adoption of the metric system of weights and measures for the United States and recommends that the units of that system be used by scientific men in all their publications."

Comparative advantages of the metric system are greatest for students at all levels, from the lower primary grades to postgraduate college. American children spend endless, tedious hours in elementary school learning how many inches in a foot, ounces in a pound, acres in a square mile, grains in an ounce, pecks in a bushel and so on and on—and forget most of it as soon as they are out of the schoolroom. They spend even more time learning arithmetic concepts and computations that are necessary to use the Customary System of weights and measures but otherwise are of little practical value. In a recent article in *The Arithmetic Teacher* the statement was made, "Much time is spent in learning to use vulgar fractions. The teaching of the use of eighths, sixteenths, thirty-seconds, and sixty-fourths of an inch is a disgrace and a serious handicap in obtaining an education." Most people also forget this as soon as they leave school—few adults can multiply or divide fractions with ease or assurance.

By contrast, any child of average intelligence can learn the basic elements of the metric system—the names of the common units and the principle of moving a decimal point—in a few hours and this learning is so simple that it is never forgotten. Metric advocates make much of the time that their system would save in teaching arithmetic. Some say two years in the elementary grades; the most conservative estimate is 10 percent. Regardless of which estimate is closer to the fact, there is no question that *some* teaching time would be saved that could be devoted to more valuable and constructive learning.

Those who should be considered as experts in teaching mathematics strongly endorse conversion to the metric system. The National Council of Teachers of Mathematics consider the subject so important that they devoted their entire Twentieth Yearbook to the metric system. The National Education Association, the leading educational association, passed the following resolution in 1968:

> The National Education Association recognizes the importance of the Metric System of weights and measures in contemporary world commerce and technology. The Association believes that a carefully planned effort to convert to the Metric System is essential to the future of American industrial and technological development and to the evolution of effective world communication. It supports federal legislation which would facilitate such a conversion. The

Association believes it is imperative that those who teach and those who produce instructional materials begin now to prepare for this conversion by urging teachers to emphasize the use of the Metric System in regular classroom activities.

# 5

# THE GREAT METRIC
# CONTROVERSY

The debate on whether the United States should adopt
the metric as its sole official system of weights and measures
is perhaps the world's longest nonstop argument; it has continued for over a century and a half. At times, the conflict
has quietly simmered for two or three decades, marked only
by occasional erudite papers in scientific journals. Then,
periodically, the controversy has livened to a raging boil
with opponents delivering phillipics that challenged the sanity,
morals, patriotism, and honesty of all who disagreed with
them.

A phenomenon of the argument has been the almost hys-
terical emotionalism that some participants have displayed.
It would seem that metrology, as a subject of debate, would
have no emotional appeal. It is, after all, an application of
mathematics and one would expect the arguments to be on
a cool, reasoned, factual plane. Instead, the metric system
has inspired more intense and virulent prose than an attack
on the sanctity of motherhood. In stormy Congressional hearings, witnesses have shouted charges of lying, fraud, deceit,
ignorance, stupidity, and a malign purpose to enslave the
country to foreigners. Most of this has been on the part of the
antimetrics, many of whom have defended their beliefs with
the ardor of zealots. The principal leadership of the pros has

always been among scientists and educators, who at times have seemed rather confused by the tempests that their opinions have unleashed.

But no antimetric went so far as metric proponent Col. Manley R. Gibson, who dedicated his life for 20 years after his retirement from the army to selling the idea that the adoption of the metric system would bring about better international accord. Discouraged by his lack of progress in two decades, Col. Gibson recently hanged himself in the basement of his San Francisco home, leaving a note to the Internal Revenue Service in which he said, "I have spent all my money and insurance loans to establish the metric system in the United States. My death should be in full payment."

Had Congress acted when the country was young, it would have been a relatively simple matter to adopt the metric system. The cost would have been negligible and the disruption to the economy of a small agricultural country and in the lives of its people very slight; not as great, probably, as the change from pounds, shillings, and pence to dollars, quarters, and dimes. There was no organized opposition at that time; no pressure on Congress from elements with selfish reasons for maintaining the status quo. But the legislators paid no heed to Jefferson's suggestion for a radical revision to put weights and measures on a decimal basis, nor to Adams' later recommendation for the "ultimate establishment of universal and permanent uniformity." When it would have been easy to change, the United States stayed with the system it had inherited from England largely through apathy and inertia.

The great metric controversy started early in the 19th century, when a few scientists, educators, and other well-informed individuals advanced the proposal that America should change to the French system, which, they claimed, was much simpler and vastly superior to the English system. They were promptly labeled as godless men. A principal argument against the metric system during much of the 19th century was on religious grounds. Everybody knew, said metric opponents, that the French were atheists. At the same time that the new system of weights and measures had come into being they had adopted a new calendar that abolished the Sabbath. This decimal calender, which lasted for 14 years, had weeks of 10 days with no provision for a weekly holy day.

This attack on the godless basis of the metric system was never moderate.

> This system came out of the "Bottomless Pit." At that time and in the place whence this system sprang it was hell on earth. The people defied the God who made them; they worshipped the Goddess of reason. In their mad fanaticism they brought forth monsters—unclean things. Can you, the children of the Pilgrim Fathers, worship at such a shrine, and force upon your brethren the untimely monster of such an age and such a place? . . . Now, my friends, when the gravediggers begin to measure our last resting places by the metric system, then understand that the curse of the Almighty may crush it just as he did the impious attempt to abolish the Sabbath.

The Francophobes who believed the French to be ungodly were not all ignorant people. Many in high places saw a denial of the Deity in the writings of the same French philosophers who had created the metric system. When the Library of Congress was destroyed by the British sack of Washington, D.C., in 1814, Thomas Jefferson offered to sell his personal library to the government for a pittance as the nucleus of a new collection. Debate in Congress as to whether his offer should be accepted was long and heated, for it was known that he had some books that expressed the new French thinking. His offer was accepted only with the stipulation that, when his library was received in Washington, a committee was "to select therefrom all books of an atheistical, irreligious, and immoral tendency, if any such there were, and send them back to Mr. Jefferson."

This involvement of religion with metrology lasted until nearly the end of the 19th century. An aspect of it, other than supposed French atheism, was the theory that Anglo-Saxon weights and measures had been Divinely ordained and to tamper with them would be sacrilegious. Some supported this belief by pointing out that Anglo-American units were derived from the cubit, which was mentioned by God when he gave Noah the specifications for the Ark. Others based their contention on the relation of the foot and other linear units to parts of the human body, which had been divinely designed, their measurements therefore being sacred. Nobody seems to have pointed out that the base 10 on which the decimal system was founded probably came from man counting on his fingers the number of which was also divinely ordained.

This religious defense of the Anglo-American units of weights and measures reached its apogee in the 1880's, when a society was established called The International Institute for Preserving and Perfecting Weights and Measures. It proclaimed: "We believe our work to be of God; we are actuated by no selfish nor mercenary motive. We depreciate personal antagonism of every kind, but we proclaim a ceaseless antagonism to the great evil, the French Metric System." The Institute further stated that "The inch, being one five-hundred-millionth of the earth's polar diameter, and in use by the people of God from the remotest antiquity, is of Divine origin, and therefore not to be displaced by man's invention."

The Institute went off on something of a tangent in its defense of the Customary System of weights and measures by involving them with the Pyramid of Cheops. It published a magazine with the resounding title, *The International Standard—devoted to the discussion and dissemination of the wisdom contained in the Great Pyramid of Jeezah in Egypt.* The pyramid premise stemmed from the 19th chapter of Isaiah, in which it was said, "In that day there shall be an altar to Jehovah in the midst of the land of Egypt, and a pillar at the border thereof to Jehovah; and it shall be for a sign and for a witness to Jehovah of hosts in the land of Egypt."

This altar, said *The International Standard*, was the Great Pyramid of which the dimensions had been ordained by God and were therefore sacred—and the key dimension of the pyramid was the Anglo-Saxon inch: "The true Pyramid is the pure, exact model of cosmic structure, and it carries in its theorem the similitude of all cosmic metrology."

The Institute people were extreme Anglo-Saxon chauvinists. They connected Joseph with the pyramid, either as its builder or its occupant, and claimed that two sons fathered by Joseph in Egypt were the leaders of the lost tribes of Israel, who had led their followers northward to become the Anglo-Saxons. The English and their American cousins were therefore God's chosen people, destined to rule the world. Because of the Divine sponsorship of the Anglo-Saxons, their weights and measures were sacred. *The International Standard* made this clear in an editorial addressed

> To the educators of Anglo-Saxondom who are ignorantly trying to force the metric system upon the youth of the country:
>
> How can you, as good citizens and heirs of the wisdom of past ages, attempt to overthrow the weights and measures that have been handed down to you from time immemorial. . . . Do you understand the origin of our own weights and measures? Have you studied their antiquity, their relation to the cosmos? Do you understand what we propose to accept instead? . . . You ought to know that the acceptance of the French metric system implies the utter overthrow of the Anglo-Saxon. You might as logically propose to substitute the French language for your mother tongue, and if you can read the signs of the times you must know that Anglo-Saxon is to be the language of the world. You propose to give up your birthright without inquiring what it is. You are as bad as Esau. Do you know that there were hundreds of thousands of arrests and fines in France to enforce the French metre? Do you know that the same class of men who compelled its adoption burnt the Bible, thinking that they could destroy the Divine evidence of the origin of our weights and measures by destroying the book?

A condemnation of the metric system based on a combination of religion and chauvinism was expressed in a song published in *The International Standard*—and elsewhere—entitled *A Pint's a Pound the World Around*. Following are two of its five stanzas and the chorus:

> *They bid us change the ancient "names,"*
> *The "seasons" and the "times,"*
> *And for our measures go abroad*
> *To strange and distant climes.*
> *But we'll abide by things long dear,*
> *And cling to things of yore,*
> *For the Anglo-Saxon race shall rule*
> *The earth from shore to shore.*
>
> *Then down with every "metric" scheme*
> *Taught by the foreign school.*
> *We'll worship still our* Father's *God!*
> *And keep our Father's "rule"!*
> *A perfect inch, a perfect pint,*
> *The Anglo's honest pound,*
> *Shall hold their place upon the earth,*
> *Till Time's last trump shall sound!*
>
> *Then swell the chorus heartily,*
> *Let every Saxon sing:*
> *"A pint's a pound the world around,"*
> *Till all the earth shall ring,*
> *"A pint's a pound the world around"*
> *For rich and poor the same:*
> *Just measure and a perfect weight*
> *Called by their ancient name!*

When it was learned that the meter was not a true tenmillionth of the quarter meridian on which it was based the antimetric forces leaped on this with unholy glee. One of the major claims for the metric system was that it was scientific and now it was apparent that there was nothing scientific about the meter. The inch, the foot, and the yard had natural relationships to parts of the human body; but the meter was merely an arbitrary unit having no direct relationship with anything. Further, the meter was based on a quadrant of a meridian, a curved line. Who but the devious French, asked metric opponents, would base a straight linear unit of measure on part of a circle?

Another antimetric argument was that the system had never been adopted in any country voluntarily; the change had everywhere been the subject of government edict, frequently with penalties provided in the form of fines for using other than metric units in legal or official transactions or, in some cases, in trade. Zealots in the opposition camp always referred to the oppressive and tyrannical nature of the Old World governments that ordained the new system; and mentioned its enforcement at the points of bayonets and the jails that bulged with offenders. Actually, there is no record of the use of force in converting to the metric system, nor is there any instance of a violator going to jail, unless he sold by a short measure, metric or otherwise. The punitive aspects of metric laws have seldom been enforced, particularly in the case of retail transactions.

This part of the law governing weights and measures in metric countries is largely concerned with *accurate* metric measures, and in this respect is similar to a number of federal laws in the United States that provide fiscal penalties for failure to use containers that exactly meet government standards. For instance, under the "Standard Barrel Act" of 1915, one may be fined for not using a barrel of 7,056 cubic inches "for fruits, vegetables, and other dry commodities other than cranberries." Proponents of the metric system point to many compulsory laws dealing with weights and measures in the United States, rather than the single law of most metric countries. Further, they point out that no people who were compelled to adopt the metric system by government edict ever sought to return to their previous system after they became familiar with the metric.

The antimetric arguments that were most prevalent in the 18th century were summed up by one writer thusly:

1. The French metric system is unscientific.
2. It is founded on a curved line instead of a straight line.

3. It is based on the particular meridian of Paris, of the infinite number.
4. It is inaccurate and untrue, as now admitted.
5. It is inharmonious with nature.
6. It is bi-lingual.
7. Its terms are cumbersome and long.
8. Its unit of length is not a natural stride, and has no reference to personal measures.
9. It is offensive in its religious relations.
10. It is not in consonance with, and is farthest removed from, scriptural and sacred systems of weights and measures, of all known systems.
11. The adoption of the French system by us would be practically and profoundly oppressive.

Chauvinism has come down to the present as a prime argument of some metric system opponents—perhaps the most widely used one. They say that because the metric system is foreign, it cannot be as good as an American system. America is the greatest country in the world, therefore its system of weights and measures must be the greatest. America pioneered in building the most precise machinery and the rest of the world turns to the United States as the acknowledged source of such machinery; and this machinery was and is built to and operates on inch dimensions. Therefore the inch must be the best system for precise work.

In fact, the dependence of the rest of the world on American machinery is steadily decreasing. American manufacturers are meeting increasingly stiff competition from metric products of Russian, Czech, German, and Japanese competitors. It is estimated that about 74 percent of the world's machine tools now operate on the metric system.

Although American machinery and industrial devices are built to the inch system, those that are used for fine work are usually calibrated decimally. Most verniers, micrometers, and other precision instruments are graduated in tenths, hundredths, thousandths, and ten-thousandths of an inch. Machinists' scales are generally graduated decimally along one edge and by binary fractions down to one sixty-fourth along another. For measurements finer than one sixty-fourth, decimal divisions are almost universally used. This weakens the argument that the inch system is preferable, since to use it for fine work it is necessary to impose on it the decimal basis of the metric system.

The 100-percent Americans also condemn the metric system because the names of its units are foreign words. Why, they ask, should Americans have to learn such alien terms as centimeter and kilogram when they have such good old Anglo-Saxon names as foot and pound? They ignore the preponderance of words of Latin or Greek derivation in the English language on the grounds that these have been around for a long time and have therefore become sanctified by usage. They also ignore the fact that "mill," meaning one-thousandth, is our smallest monetary unit and "cent," meaning one-hundredth, our smallest coin; and "meter" is a very familiar word applied to instruments that measure water, gas, electricity, parking time, automobile speed, etc. Metric opponents further claim that the similarity of some of the prefixes is confusing. Deca- and deci- are the ones that they always use as examples because, in truth, these are the only ones that are similar. To a child who learns their meaning in the second grade these prefixes are no more confusing than any other two words with similar sounds.

Those who oppose the metric system make much of the fact that no country uses it exclusively. People in metric countries persist in using multiples and subdivisions of units derived through the binary rather than the decimal system of numbers. This will always be true, because for some aspects of measurements in daily life the binary system is far better than the decimal. It is easier to divide some things into halves or quarters or eighths than into tenths or direct multiples of a tenth. Any housewife can apportion a pie into 8 relatively equal pieces by dividing it in half, dividing the halves into equal quarters, and then dividing the quarters; but no one could, without measuring instruments, divide a pie into ten equal pieces; so French housewives, like American ones, divide pies into quarters and eighths.

Another premise of the antimetrics is that everybody knows the American system; why should they learn a new one? In fact, the reverse of this statement is almost true—*nobody* knows the American system. There may be some pedants with phenomenal memories who could answer any question on the 80-plus units that comprise the American system of weights and measures—but they are rare indeed. Most Americans know a few units and ignore the rest. They recognize a quart milk bottle, a 5-gallon can, and, perhaps, a bushel basket. To most Americans, a quart is what goes in the bottle and a bushel is what goes in the basket. These are measures of capacity, and virtually no one knows what their capacity is. None but specialists in certain fields knows the exact meaning of most measures in the American system. A surveyor knows what a rod is, a mariner comprehends a fathom, a pharmacist could define a scruple, and all horse-players understand a furlong; but to most Americans, these are terms that they learned in school and promptly forgot.

Antimetrics ask, What difference does it make? Most people can go through life quite contentedly without rods, fathoms, furlongs, scruples, and drams. But, claim the prometrics, is it not rather ridiculous to have many little groups of people who use their own special measurements when it could all be done so much more simply and easily by one unified system?

A simple, short test will serve to demonstrate that virtually nobody except a student of metrology actually knows the system of weights and measures under which Americans live, for one would journey long and far before finding anyone who could answer all these questions:

1. A bushel and a gallon are defined in terms of their capacity in cubic inches. How many cubic inches are there in a bushel? In a gallon?
2. An acre is a measure of square feet or square rods. How

many square feet are there in an acre? How many square rods?

3. How many acres are there in a square mile?
4. What is the difference in capacity between a liquid quart and a dry quart?
5. How many pecks are there in a bushel? How many quarts in a peck?
6. How many quarts are there in a barrel? (Nobody could answer this one; it depends on what is in the barrel and whether it is used as a dry or liquid measure. There are several different barrels defined by U.S. statutes.)
7. How many cubic inches are there in a cubic yard? (Many people could undoubtedly calculate this in time, but few could give the answer offhand.)

Any school child in a metric country could provide the answer to questions such as these merely by moving decimal points.

The meter has been subjected to much criticism by anti-metrics for reasons other than its nonscientific basis. Some say that it is possible to pace off yards with a fair degree of accuracy whereas one cannot readily pace off meters. This, say the prometrics, is merely a matter of opinion. Since a pace is dependent on the length of the pacer's legs, a tall man may pace off meters more readily than he can pace off yards; and most women cannot pace off either. In any event, most people cannot pace off yards with an accuracy within 10 percent, and this is roughly the difference between the length of a yard and a meter.

A somewhat more valid argument is that the meter is too long to represent a handy unit for many day-to-day measuring tasks; the foot is more convenient. It is also claimed that the decimeter is too long to take the place of an inch and the centimeter too short. This is true so long as one thinks in terms of inches, feet, and yards. If one thinks in terms of metric divisions, 30 centimeters is just as handy as one foot and 25 millimeters is just as handy as one inch. These are the nearest round number equivalents to American measures. Thirty-centimeter hand rulers, divided into millimeters, are as commonplace in metric countries as one-foot rulers are in the United States. There is little more than a quarter-inch difference between them.

The flare-ups in the controversy regarding the adoption of the metric system have usually paralleled sporadic Congressional interest in the subject. Bills to make the metric system the only official system of the United States, to have it exclusively adopted by government departments, or merely to study the whole subject of weights and measures have been periodically introduced in the Congress. During the last half of the 19th century, there were 14 such bills and one House resolution; during the first 3 decades of the present century there were at least 36. Most of the bills have died in committee, many without formal hearings. The principal flurries of controversy revolved around bills that were introduced in the 1880's, in 1902, and the early 1920's.

The closest that the United States ever came to adopting the metric system was in 1902. But for an unexpected adjournment of the first session of that year's Congress, a bill would have been passed requiring all government departments to use the system exclusively. The bill was introduced by Congressman Southard of Ohio. When it came before his Committee on Weights and Measures, it was endorsed by a parade of impressive witnesses from the fields of science, education, and the military. Petitions piled up from scientific and technical societies and resolutions from several state legislatures supporting the bill.

Southard's bill was unanimously approved by his committee and the debate was set for early in July, 1902. It was a foregone conclusion that the bill would pass. Said a Milwaukee newspaper, "It is as sure as anything in the future can be sure." The *New York Times,* one of the few papers opposed to the bill, admitted that it would certainly pass by a large majority.

Congress had remained in session so late in the summer

of 1902 because the important question of terminating military rule in Cuba was to come before it. Then a change on the diplomatic front deferred this, and there was a motion to adjourn before the date set for the metric debate. Southard did not object; the metric question had been around for a long time and waiting a few months for the second session would not make any difference.

By the time Congress had reconvened, some opposition to the bill had developed. The textile and shoe industries had protested on the grounds of the cost of conversion, and a man named Frederick A. Halsey, editor of the *American Machinist,* had launched a crusade against it with fiery editorials denouncing the integrity of those who favored the metric system. This attack ignored the true purpose of the bill, which was to make the metric system mandatory only within the government. Halsey led people to believe that the bill, if it became law, would wipe out the Customary System of weights and measures overnight and lead to chaos and repressive, bureaucratic domination of their lives. The intemperance of the attack and the personal charges that were part of it distressed Southard to the point that he withdrew his bill in mid-session, although a press poll of Congress showed that it still had an ample majority on the floor.

Southard's purpose in withdrawing the bill was to give its supporters time to properly explain it and correct the misconceptions that Halsey had created. By the time that he reintroduced it in a later Congress, the opposition had established a strong lobby supported by elements of industry. If the government had changed to metric measures many manufacturers who sought government contracts would perforce have had to go along. Few manufacturers were willing to pay the short-term cost of conversion, so their lobbyists pressured legislators to drag their feet on the metric bill. It needed only five votes in committee to keep the bill from coming to the floor and the lobbyists were always able to influence this small number.

One of the most respected witnesses when Southard's bill

was reintroduced in 1906 was Alexander Graham Bell, who gave a lengthy dissertation on the merits of the metric system, presenting the Congressmen with several problems in calculation that they could not do and then showing them how simply they could be done under the metric system. Apparently, Bell did not use the metric system in inventing the telephone; he introduced it in his laboratory in connection with his later work in aeronautics. In trying to calculate the relation between wind force and the weight of his experimental kites, "the calculations proved to be so laborious that I found it simpler to translate the proposed measurements into metrical terms and then work out the solution on the metrical plan."
Bell then completely converted his laboratory to metrics.

> The result may be of interest to the committee as bearing upon the question of the ability of the common people of America to handle a new system of this kind. No difficulty whatever was experienced in the use of the system, and the total expense involved in the change amounted to a few dollars for the purchase of a set of metrical weights and measures. The same balances formerly employed were equally efficient in weighing by the metrical system, and even the old weights were utilized as supplementary weights, with their value in grams distinctly marked upon them. No change was required in the machinery and tools employed, simply a change in the method of measuring the output.

Bell claimed that the problem of retraining his workmen was negligible.

> All the difficulties in the metric system are in translating from one system to the other, but the moment you use the metric system alone there is no difficulty. The workmen in my laboratory used the metrical weights and measures right off. I did not ask them to translate from one system to the other, for that would speedily have developed their limitations of education. I simply asked them to use the metric system, and they did it without difficulty. They now use meters and centimeters and grams and kilograms as if to

the manner born, and they are simply common carpenters and mechanics. I consider them as an average sample of the common people. I do not anticipate any difficulty in the use of the metric system by itself.

When asked about the cost of conversion Bell replied:

I think that the difficulty has been unduly magnified. The fact is that the change does not necessarily involve any change in tools or machinery at all—or at least not to any great extent. It is a question of arithmetic, not of tools or machinery. You can measure the work or output of the present tools or machinery just as well by the metric system as in the ordinary way. . . . It is only where very fine and accurate measurements are required that special tools would be needed.

As to the charge that the inch was more convenient than the centimeter, Bell said, "This was merely a matter of usage; to those familiar with the centimeter, judgment was just the other way." For practical daily use, all people really had to know were the meter, the kilogram, and the liter, and, to convert, remember that the meter was about one-tenth more than the yard, the liter about one-twentieth more than the quart, and the kilogram one-tenth more than two pounds.

The metric issue again came before Congress in the early 1920's, when hearings on another bill for government conversion were held by a Senate committee. The situation was quite different than it had been in 1902. In the interim, there had been a vast expansion in American industry. Big Business had become the order of the day and new industries had been born or come of age. America was industry-minded as she had not been in the 19th century, and the views of industry had compelling influence.

Both sides in the great metric controversy were better organized in the 1920's than they had been previously. The World Metric Standardization Council presented its case in a 525-page book with the theme, "Keep the World War Won." It pointed out that the United States Army had adopted the metric system for wartime use in France and claimed that this evidenced a compelling need for a universal world system. The Council claimed that "the German Kaiser would not have dared declare war if America and the British Commonwealth had been standardized on metrics." Most of this book was devoted to proving the strength of the metric advocates. Hundreds of pages listed names of prominent individuals, associations, professional men, Chambers of Commerce, and individual businesses who favored the metric system. The metric advocates have always had a virtual monopoly on "big names," particularly in science and education.

The antimetric forces also had a book in the form of a research report from the National Industrial Conference Board. This organization is supported by business and industry and its investigation was largely limited to these areas. It claimed that its report "presents accurate and comprehensive information on the subject and gives an impartial synopsis of the arguments on both sides." Actually, there was nothing impartial about the report; it was a brief for the retention of the Customary System. It expressed the contentions of the metric advocates in a few words and then presented, at much greater length, opinion, evidence, and statistics to disprove them.

A principal argument of metric proponents was that their system, with its small number of units, is basically simpler because all units are interrelated and divided or multiplied by the decimal system. The report answered this by claiming that the Anglo-American system had developed from a natural selection of the fittest units for particular uses and not as a result of a rigid inflexible plan; and that the American system used decimal computation for certain limited needs where it best applied, but also used the binary and duodecimal systems far more extensively because they were better in most cases.

Most of the report merely represented an expression of conflicting opinion, with the businessmen and industrialists whom the Conference Board interviewed politely calling the scientists and educators liars. Metric proponents claimed that conversion could be accomplished gradually without much confusion; opponents insisted any change would "produce a long aftermath during which the mechanical industries of the country would suffer from tremendous confusion." Metric proponents maintained that there was "a strong and growing demand for a change to the metric system in this country among all classes of people." Opponents denied "that there is any demand worthy of serious consideration . . . and that what little demand exists comes from teachers, scientists, and a few others representing . . . not more than one tenth of one percent of the country." The implication was that metric advocates were a bunch of eggheads who did not know the facts of life and should keep the metric system in their ivory towers.

Metric proponents claimed that there was "a growing realization that the English system is crude and confusing and that the adoption of the metric system would eliminate this confusion and secure world uniformity." Opponents insisted "that this is absolutely false." They countered that there was no confusion, and that, "on the contrary, there is increasing indication that the English system, with slight modifications, is coming to be fully realized as the ideal system." Metric proponents, pointing to the experience in other countries, claimed that "the people of the United States would adopt the new units without serious confusion after a relatively short transition period." Opponents flatly denied that other countries had made the change simply and easily and contended that, "even where a substantial degree of uniformity exists in a metric country, today, the experience of all metric countries proves that a long transition period ranging from twenty-five to one hundred years is necessarily involved in making a change in systems."

And so it went. Metric advocates claimed that the cost of transition would be negligible over a protracted period. Their opponents insisted that the change would "entail the discarding or alteration of a large part of the basic mechanical equipment of the manufacturing industries of the countries . . . the only result . . . would be to drag the country into an enormous expenditure and waste without providing any compensatory advantages." By a system of accounting that was not explained, the National Industrial Conference Board figured out that conversion to the metric system would cost American business and industry some $200 per employee.

The Conference Board report admitted that a universal system would have some advantage in foreign trade, but advanced statistics to prove that but an infinitesimal percentage of the population was concerned with foreign trade. Further, they pointed out, again with statistics, 56.6 percent of America's foreign trade was with nonmetric countries, principally the British Commonwealth. "The facts indicate that the trade of the world is not carried on more in the metric system than it is in the English and that, as a matter of fact, the English system predominates."

The Conference Board report advanced as a compelling argument against the universality of the metric system a list of industries in metric countries that continued to use the Anglo-American system. In the textile industry, English yarn counts were used in practically every country. In metal products, English machine standards based on the inch predominated even in metric countries. In the lumber industry, the inch-foot system prevailed almost universally in board sizes. In paper and printing type, sizes had been standardized in most countries on the basis of the inch. In the chemical industry, the machinery employed was made largely to English measurements even in metric countries.

In the United States, claimed the report, there was decided opposition to the metric system throughout all industry. The textile industry was quoted as being completely satisfied with the present system. The metal industry voted over 90 percent against the metric system. The food products, lumber, paper and printing, automobile, railway, shipbuilding, and implement industries "also went on record as decidedly averse to any change."

Senator McNary, who presided over the hearings in the early 1920's, complained of the difficulty of keeping witnesses to the subject. There was heated debate on such matters as the percentage of the Mexican railroad system that had converted to the metric system, or how rice was weighed in Burma. Witnesses flatly contradicted each other and frequently the discussions became heated and highly personal. Witnesses representing business and industry talked at length about their concern for the welfare of mankind and the rights of free Americans; but after all the bombast it was apparent they were all opposed to the metric system for one reason— it would be costly to change and they did not want to spend the money.

In all, most people, including a great many national and world organizations, supported the metric system and relatively few opposed it—only about one percent of the 100,000-plus petitions received by the legislative committee were antimetric —but the Senate committee did not report favorably on the bill because of prejudice and pressure. The first was expressed in the fanatical opposition of antimetric zealots; the second, and far more important, factor was the strength of well-financed industrial lobbies. Metric proponents had no lobby. During the boom of the twenties few Senators would flout the wishes of industry in a matter about which their constituents knew little and cared less.

The opposition of the metric system was summarized in a series of articles in *Forbes* magazine in 1924 by a writer named Joseph Mayer, who was still campaigning vigorously against the adoption of the system in the 1960's. Most of the arguments presented in this series were the hoary clichés of the 18th century, except that the religious aspect was not mentioned. The English system, said the writer, was traditional, everybody understood it; the United States led the world in standardization, the interchangeability of parts, etc., and this was done under the English system—therefore this system must be better; the metric system was not scientific because the supposed natural basis of the meter was incorrect;

the English system was based on handy lengths and ready measures found in nature; the metric system was rigid and inflexible because of its strict adherence to the decimal system for all calculations; the English system was more flexible because it contained "binary, tertiary, decimal, and duo-decimal divisibility"; the binary method was the easiest mode of division; the weakness of the metric system was proven by the fact that old units were still in use in countries that had adopted the metric system many years ago.

The prometric argument that the adoption of this system would stimulate foreign trade was doubly refuted—foreign trade represented only some 5 percent of the commerce of the United States, and over half of it was with countries that were predominantly nonmetric. The only ones who would benefit by a change were a few exporters and foreign manufacturers in metric countries who sought to sell their products in the United States—this last point, that the change would benefit foreigners, was italicized. The thousands of petitions that Congress had received favoring the metric system were brushed off by the claim that these represented *all* metric proponents and that they were, in the main, a bunch of intellectuals or crackpots. The only supporters of the metric system were scientists, fine instrument makers, exporters, and a few edu-cators who comprised less than one-tenth of one percent of the population and who were trying to coerce the remaining 99.9 percent of the people into the compulsory use of the pernicious metric system.

The series of articles summarized above was typical of all antimetric propaganda, and it must be admitted that the metric opponents were better demagogues than the advocates of the system. Although most of their arguments were shallow or fallacious, they had much popular appeal. The contention that the Customary System should be retained because it is "traditional" is reminiscent of a prophecy that was often heard in the early days of the automobile: "It will never replace the horse." The unscientific basis of the meter has nothing to do with the merits of either system, nor has the natural derivations of units in the English system. To one who thinks in terms of metric units, the quart is no handier than the liter, the foot no handier than 30 centimeters, the mile no handier than the kilometer. The fact that old units were still in use in metric countries—that the Germans loved their pfund—had no bearing on the subject. The contention that the metric system is inflexible because it is based exclusively on decimal arithmetic is fallacious because, in metric countries, the binary system of numbers is used where it is more applicable —people still cut things in half and it makes no difference whether they call the result .5 or ½. *Every* mathematician agrees that the decimal system is basically easier and less prone to error for most calculations and that the binary system is better for some practical, everyday measurements.

The fact that America led the world in standardization has no bearing on the relative merits of measuring systems; products can be standardized equally well under either system. The argument that most of America's foreign trade was with nonmetric countries no longer applies; today, over 75 percent of all world production and trade is in the metric system, and, after its adoption by the British Commonwealth, virtually all international commerce will be with metric countries.

A popular technique among opponents of the adoption of the metric system is to assume that a law making the system compulsory would require that total change be made immediately and to then stress the complete chaos that would result from such a change. Replacement parts on machines would not interchange with existing parts, for many years all inventories of parts would have to be in duplicate; metric bolts would not fit inch-system holes; metric pipe would not connect with inch pipe; all technical literature and reference handbooks would have to be rewritten and metric dimensions would have to be added to all existing working drawings. To change from miles to kilometers it would be necessary to replace all speed limit and distance road signs and all railroad distance markers. To denote a speed limit of 40 miles per hour, a new sign would read "Speed limit 64.374 kilometers per hour." This would not make sense so the speed limit would be changed to 65 kilometers an hour; a change that would necessitate revising all of the speed laws. The dials on every automobile speedometer would have to be replaced.

All existing tape measures, yardsticks, and engineering tapes would have to be replaced. All cook books would need to be rewritten and all kitchen measuring devices would become obsolete. All measures of capacity and all computing scales would become illegal—every quart bottle, gallon can, and bushel basket would have to be replaced. Every gas and water meter and every gasoline pump would have to be recalibrated. All laws relating to such things as easements and width of roads would have to be revised. All real estate deeds and plots would have to be expressed in new dimensions. All historical data, such as those compiled by the Bureau of the Census, would have to be converted.

This argument has great popular appeal, although it has little to do with reality in many of the areas mentioned. Even the most prometric fanatics have never recommended a crash program of conversion. In every country that has converted, the change has been a gradual one over a period of years. England is trying to make the change, on the industrial front, in a decade, and if this is accomplished it will be a shorter period than was required in any other highly developed country.

In many areas, only a change in language is required to convert—present measurements can be expressed in the metric system as well as in the inch-pound system. In other areas, things may be converted to the new system when they wear out, become obsolete, or require reconditioning. Road signs giving distances must be frequently repainted. Without additional expense, distances in kilometers could be added to the signs together with distances in miles. Mileages could remain for several years until people became familiar with the new measure.

Metric advocates admit that, for a time, there will necessarily be costly duplication—literature and working drawings in dual dimensions, etc. Duplicate replacement parts are not new to industry; manufacturers continue to make parts for old models that have been changed in new models so long as the old models are in general use. This practice would be expanded by conversion, but proponents of change maintain that the temporary cost and confusion would be more than compensated for by the ultimate economy and simplicity of the metric system.

Important in the great metric controversy during the early years of the 20th century was the conflict between scientists and engineers. At that time, the laboratory work of scientists did not have such extensive and immediate application in industry as it has today, nor was easy communication between scientists and technicians so necessary. Except in a few industries, such as the chemical and electrical, the work of scientists—other than inventions—was not considered as having much practical value; it was the engineer who designed and built the products and structures on which America's leadership was based. Few questioned the fact that the metric system was preferable for laboratory work, but engineers, who had never learned the metric system, maintained that it had no particular value in the factory or on the construction site. The opinions of the engineers were not objective since they only knew one system, but they carried a great deal more weight than the views of the scientists in an era that was more oriented toward engineering and production. This conflict goes to the root of the controversy. Metric measures are unquestionably simpler and more accurate for *computation,* and this figures large in the work of scientists. The Customary System is satisfactory for most *measurement,* a matter that is of more concern to engineers.

Some metric proponents have made much of the fact that all units in this system are interrelated; units of weight and capacity are based on a linear unit, the meter. Antimetrics have shrugged this off, claiming that it has no practical value —what difference does it make whether a quart and a pound are related to a foot? Extremists have even claimed that it is not true. In the articles quoted above the statement was made that "A liter of oats, cannon balls, chicken feathers, potatoes or strawberries will have different weights due to their difference in specific gravities, and none of these liters will weigh a kilogram." The fallacy here, of course, is that the liter is a unit of capacity, not a unit of weight. If oats, cannon balls, etc., are sold by weight they are not measured by the liter.

The true value of the interrelationship of various measuring units in the metric system is that there is only one basic unit in each area and this is used for all measurements in that area. Anything that is considered in terms of capacity, be it liquid or dry, is measured in terms of divisions or multiples of a liter—a cubic decimeter. Anything that is considered in terms of weight is measured by divisions or multiples of a gram— the equivalent of a cubic centimeter of water at a certain temperature. Under the Customary System, there are different measures of capacity that bear no logical relation to each other for different substances. Examples are the gallon and the bushel. True, the gallon and the bushel can be related in terms of weight, the former being a vessel containing 8.3389 pounds of water at a given temperature and pressure and the latter a measure containing 77.6274 pounds of water under the same conditions, but the relationship is purely arbitrary. In weights, there are three different units for different purposes—avoirdupois, troy, and apothecary. Further, the bushel, a measure of capacity, is almost universally used as a measure of weight. Since the weight of a given capacity of a substance depends on its density there is a considerable difference in the weight of bushels of various commodities, necessitating a multiplicity of laws on the subject. By legal definition, a bushel of oats weighs 32 pounds, a bushel of wheat 60 pounds, a bushel of corn 56 pounds, etc.

Another point of dispute in the great metric controversy is the effect of adopting the system on the teaching of arithmetic in terms of time and costs. The former chairman of the mathematics department of Chicago Teachers College claims that two years of elementary arithmetic could be eliminated from the grade school program if the United States dropped the conventional system of measure, with its overemphasis on fractions, in favor of the metric system. The antimetrics deny this and claim the adoption of the system would materially increase the time and cost of teaching arithmetic because, for a generation at least, it would be necessary to teach both systems; the training necessitated by the metric system would be superimposed on the present curriculum.

Floyd W. Hough, chairman of the American Geophysical Union Study of the Metric System, made the statement that

> Teachers of mathematics will agree that fully 25 percent of the child's time, and the teacher's time as well, could be saved in arithmetic courses if the simple, interrelated metric decimal units were substituted for the English system of measure. Such monstrosities as proper and improper fractions, numerators, least common denominators, greatest common divisors, and mixed numbers could be laid to rest with the celluloid collar and the oxcart.

Fred J. Helgren, President of the Metric Association, used this estimate as partial documentation for a computation of the saving in dollars that could be effected by the elimination of the teaching of arithmetic necessary to the Customary System. Wrote Mr. Helgren:

> The average cost to educate a pupil in the grade schools of the United States is $500 per year. Arithmetic studies use 12 percent of the pupil's and the teacher's time and costs $60 per year. If the pupil were required to study only the metric system with the resulting decrease in the study of fractions and the elimination of complex units of measure, 25 percent of the time devoted to arithmetic studies could be saved. This is a saving of $15 per pupil per year. There are 47 million pupils in the public and parochial schools of the United States. A $15 yearly saving per pupil is a national saving of 705 million dollars a year.

Mr. Helgren then went on to compare this saving with one

particular estimate of $11 billion as the cost of converting to the metric system and showed that this cost would be covered in less than 16 years by the saving in teaching arithmetic.

Mr. Helgren's estimate was made in the 1960's and the savings would be greater today, when the average annual per-pupil cost of grade school education is well over $500 and there are more pupils. However, this computation fails to take into account the undeniable fact that proper and improper fractions and least common denominators could not be dropped from the arithmetic curriculum overnight, nor would they ever be entirely eliminated. One crusty antimetric witness growled that kids should be taught fractions whether they used them or not. "It's good training for them."

One study that may have some validity in the field of education was made by UNESCO a few years ago. This survey was made among 13-year-olds in 12 European countries and disclosed that the educational achievement of English school children was significantly below that of children in other countries studied. The disparity was attributed to the excessive use of fractions and outmoded units in the British schools. The UNESCO report concludes, "It is likely to be a blow to the entrenched supporters of fractions, pounds, shillings and pence and complicated systems of measurement. We seem, in fact, to be penalizing our children by holding them to an out-of-date system."

Adding further confusion to the great metric controversy are many proposals to decimalize the Customary System to a greater or lesser extent as a compromise between ignoring and adopting the metric system. Some of these proposals would radically change the present system to create a 10-inch foot and a 10-ounce pound; others merely propose to further extend existing decimalization by using decimal instead of duodecimal or binary divisions more frequently.

In fact, the Customary System has already been decimalized to a considerable degree in operations where decimal numbers are more convenient. If we are concerned only with measurements of length to moderate precision it is convenient to express these measurements in feet, inches, and binary fractions of an inch; thus, 9 feet 4½ inches. But if such measured lengths are to be used in calculations of area or volume, this method of subdivision becomes extremely inconvenient. Civil engineers, who are concerned with measurements of land, volume of cuts, fills, excavations, etc., ordinarily express dimensions decimally in tenths, hundredths, or thousandths of a foot. The odometer portion of an automobile speedometer shows mileage in terms of tenths of a mile. In all work where precision measurements of short distances are important the inch is divided decimally to tenths, hundredths, thousandths, etc.

In measurements of capacity or weight, the decimal system is usually more convenient than any other and is gradually being used more extensively. On the dials of modern gasoline pumps, gallon divisions are in tenths rather than halves and quarters. Most supermarkets decimalize the pound in marking and pricing meat, vegetables, and some dairy products. This has caused no confusion—in fact, it has resulted in a minor saving to the housewife. When meat was weighed and priced to the nearest ounce, the butcher invariably considered a fractional ounce as a full ounce; if a steak weighed 4 pounds 6½ ounces, the buyer was charged for 4 pounds 7 ounces or, possibly, for 4½ pounds. With the new system, the price is computed exactly to one one-hundredth of a pound.

Other proposals have suggested a more radical reform by changing the base of the decimal system, usually to 12 instead of 10, although some scholars who advocate change have made a case for 8 as the base number and bemoan the fact that when man first counted on his fingers he included the thumbs. A weakness of the decimal system is that 10 is divisible only by 5 and 2, and division into thirds or quarters involves mixed numbers. Under a decimal system with a base of twelve—which is divisible by 2, 3, 4, and 6—a sixth, a quarter, a third, and a half could be expressed by whole numbers.

There have been numerous other suggested compromises

to an outright adoption of the metric system. One put forth in a recent article in *Mechanical Engineering* would retain the familiar names of the present system and gain the advantages of the metric system by changing the capacity of a quart to that of a liter, the length of a foot to 30 centimeters and the weight of a pound to 500 grams. The units would be called m-quarts, m-feet, and m-pounds. There would still be 4 quarts in an m-gallon and 12 inches in an m-foot but the inch would be 25mm instead of 25.4mm. Nothing is said about the m-ounce, which, under this proposed system, would be either 31.25g or 31.25 ml depending on whether it was used to measure a solid or a liquid. It is suggested that this system be introduced in stages, first in units of capacity, which, according to its inventor, would greatly affect only the petroleum and dairy industries. The claim is made that it "would probably spread around the world together with the metric system." This, of course, ignores the prime reason for adopting the metric system—having a single universal world system.

Except for a flurry after World War II, occasioned by the use of two systems in military production and logistics, the metric controversy was relatively dormant until 1961, when a subcommittee of the House Committee on Science and Astronautics unanimously recommended favorable action on a bill to authorize the Bureau of Standards to conduct a 3-year factual study of the pros and cons of the question. This stimulated renewed interest in the scientific and industrial press. An editorial in the June, 1962, issue of *Science* tersely expressed the arguments on both sides that were then being advanced in industry and science:

> Pro: The metric system is in universal use among scientists. Con: Scientists working with engineers who use the English system find little difficulty in converting from one system to the other, and in any case interconvertibility is no great problem since work is usually done in single units that are scaled up or down. The international inch, adopted in 1959, equals exactly 25.4 millimeters, thus simplifying conversion.
>
> Pro: The metric system permits greater speed and accu-

racy in calculations and hence great economy in time and money. Con: The main advantage of the metric system is that it is decimalized. The increasing use of the decimal inch, mile, and gallon tends to offset the advantages that the metric system has hitherto enjoyed.

Pro: The metric system is becoming the dominant system: 74 countries now use this system; 40 of them have made the shift during this century. Consequently, for full participation in world trade, it is important to use the metric system. Con: English units are in fact still in use in many metric-system countries: oil pipes and fittings, automobile tires, bicycle chains, and gears are predominantly on the inch system. What is important is not that the units of measurement be standard throughout but that there be a single standard throughout a particular industry.

Pro: The shift to the metric system is inevitable and in fact has already begun with the recent conversion of most of the American pharmaceutical manufacturers to this system, the partial conversion of the optical industry, the planned shift of the Army and Marine Corps to the metric system for all linear measures by January 1966, and the Weather Bureau's use of both systems in its maps. Con: It may be advantageous for certain industries to make the shift, but the great bulk of industry is firmly committed to the English system and has an enormous investment in drawings, gears, dies, machine and hand tools, screw threads, and so on. The cost of a shift would be astronomical, and the problem of re-educating engineers and machinists to the metric system, formidable. To shift would be to court economic disaster.

Rebuttal: The shift could be accomplished over a 33-year period and introduced only in some industries, not in all. The economic arguments against shifting are exaggerated and fail to take account of obsolescence.

Stripped of all its bombast, claims of American superiority, the misleading charges and the exaggerated assertions of zealots on both sides, the position of metric opponents may be reduced to two basic arguments. A change would be costly to industry and inconvenient to the public. Many who admit the superiority of the metric system for most purposes insist that the advantages would not be worth the tremendous cost of conversion. The Washington *Star* compared the gain versus cost situation to a man and a wife who can't stand each other but can't afford a divorce. In the matter of public convenience, the argument is that people who have spent their lives under the Customary System would find it intolerable to learn a new one. Granted that few people understand the Anglo-American system; they are quite content with what little they do know, so why change? The rebuttal to this is that people are always prejudiced in favor of things with which they are familiar and will resist change until something new proves itself. People were quite content with the horse and buggy for centuries until—over a period of almost twenty years—they became convinced that the automobile was a far superior form of transportation. Then they willingly learned to drive a car.

# 6

# HOW OTHERS CONVERTED

Countries that converted to the metric system in the 19th century did not face many of the more acute problems that would be part of a change in the United States today. The factory system was less important; things were more frequently made by craftsmen without the aid of machine tools, dies, templates, micrometers, gauges, and all the paraphernalia of modern industry that would be so costly to change. Mass production, to which interchangeability of parts is essential, was not an important factor. The precision measurements of the 20th century were rarely applied to production.

In education, the problem was the same for those early converts as it would be now in the United States; people had to learn the new system. In fact, this aspect of the change would probably be easier in the United States today because of progress in communications and universal education. In most of the countries that converted during the last century, a great many people were unreachable by any mass communications media and a sizeable proportion of the children were not exposed to regular schooling. In rural areas, there were many who had scarcely heard of the new system years after their countries had adopted it.

Most of the nations that have converted in the 20th century are primarily agrarian or were in the early stages of industrialization when the change was made. This applies to the newly emerging nations of Africa, to the countries of South America, and to such giants as Russia, China, and India. In 1927, when Russia changed to the metric system, its crash program of industrialization was just getting under way. Much of its industry started on the metric system. This is true to an even greater extent of China and India, which are still not numbered among the world's industrial giants. Because of communist secrecy, little is known about the details of conversion in China and Russia. India decided to convert in 1956 and set a target date of 10 years. Metric units of weight, capacity, and length have been the only legal units since 1963, but the changeover is still far from complete.

India had some special conversion problems, particularly metric nomenclature in the different languages used in various sections of the country. It was necessary to adopt international terminology for basic metric units. Although the inch-pound system predominated and was taught in the schools, there were local systems in some areas, and units in various systems bearing the same names differed considerably in value, in some cases by 100 percent. The change to the metric system was preceded by a conversion to decimal currency.

Metric units of weight, capacity, and length were introduced separately, each with a specific transition period of one or two years. Also, the conversion in industry was independent of, and started before, the change in retail trade and the public sector. In industry, the shortage of foreign exchange precluded the replacement of much equipment, regardless of cost. Complete conversion will involve a long transition period and no rigid timetable has been imposed. Much publicity has been given to methods of converting existing equipment and it has been found quite practicable to produce some things designed to the metric system on inch-calibrated machine tools.

Estimates of probable costs that were made before conversion started were found to be much higher than actual costs; in one extreme case—in the petroleum trade—the actual cost of changing pumps, tank calibrations, etc., was about one percent of the estimate. A study of the conversion reported, "The consensus of opinion is that cost estimates were usually highly misleading and not of great value." There were no government subsidies to ease the cost of conversion.

In retail trade and elsewhere in the public sector, most people did not act until the last moment and, although two years was allowed for the change, it was, in practice, effected within a few months. Again, there was much less confusion than anticipated. "Even kerbside traders readily adopted the new system. It was remarkable that so-called illiterates learned the new system and reconciled it with the old extremely quickly."

The introduction of the metric system in schools was also much easier than anticipated. A study reported in the organ of the British Standards Institute concluded, "It is estimated that the introduction of the metric system in primary education has saved about one year's study." The Director of the Indian Standards Institute reported:

> The use of the Metric System in schools presents little problem once the Metric System becomes a reality. . . . Our children are now learning the Metric System without the least difficulty in spite of the fact that proper text books are hard to get and also the teaching of the system is a comparatively new task for the teachers. I am mentioning this because we also thought at one time that education in schools and colleges would present serious problems. Though the change is not yet complete at all stages, we know now that the initial fears were over-exaggerated. The same remark holds good for the ordinary people. When we were debating the various issues, we heard a lot about the common man's inability to adapt himself. The common man ultimately proved to be remarkably adaptable and learned the Metric System in no time.

Japan is the only metric convert that faced problems similar to those that would face the United States. There was a span of 77 years between the time that Japan first acknowledged the metric system and the date at which she finally converted to it; and 41 years elapsed between the passage of the first law providing for the adoption of the system and the completion of conversion. However, for most of these years little effort was made to enforce the law. The active period of conversion lasted 11 years, from 1951 to 1962.

Japan's ancient system of weights and measures was based on the shaku (11.930 inches) for linear measure and the kan (8.267 pounds) as a unit of weight. After signing the international Treaty of the Meter in 1885, Japan legalized the metric system for parallel use with the traditional system, as the United States did in 1866. And, as in the United States, virtually nobody used it. As the result of the expansion of trade with England and the United States, the inch-pound system was legalized in 1909, giving Japan three systems. To deal in local products together with those imported from Europe and the United States a Japanese had to know that one kan equalled 8.267 pounds or 3.75 kilograms.

The complications caused by this triple system of measurements were so great that, in 1921, after a 2-year study, the Japanese Diet passed an act making the metric system mandatory. The enforcement date was 1924 and the law provided for a two-step transitional period, each to last ten years. The first step called for government agencies, public services, and industry to complete conversion by 1934; all other activities were supposed to convert by 1944.

Things went smoothly until the Japanese nationalists became more influential and powerful in the late 1920's. This faction saw only evil in anything from the West and maintained that the metric system was "un-Japanese." They also used arguments long familiar in the United States; change was not necessary, it was expensive, it was inconvenient, it would cause dislocations in public life, etc. As a result, conversion slowed down and it was necessary to advance the dates for its accomplishment, first by 5 years and then by 10. By 1939, opposition to the metric system had increased to the point that the law was revised to make permissible the retention of the shaku-kan system in some areas and a more distant date, 1958, was set for the completion of conversion in others. This sabotage of the development of an orderly system by the nationalists has a lesson for the United States; in favoring the old system because it was Japanese they were directly comparable to those who cry "American superiority" to support the traditional system.

After the war, which destroyed much of Japan's industrial capacity, the nation was in a position to convert almost painlessly as instruments and machine tools were replaced, but much equipment for rehabilitation came from the United States and England, bringing with it an increased utilization of the inch-pound system. Gradually, some items that had previously been made and sold by the metric system were produced by the Anglo-American system and Japan was again saddled with three separate systems.

In 1951, a new Measurement Law was passed ordaining total metric conversion by 1962. An exception was allowed in real estate, where the conversion date was 1966. By 1962, usage of the metric system was so general that a fine of $140 was established for anybody using other than metric units of measurement. The penalty has never yet been exacted.

The speed of conversion in Japan after 1951 and the relative smoothness of the operation was in part based on the fact that grade schools had started to teach the metric system in 1925. After the war, when free education was extended, teaching of metrics was further stressed so that, by the time pressure to convert was applied, an estimated 63 percent of the people were familiar with the new system.

Perhaps the most important phase of Japan's program of conversion was the work of the Metric System Promotion Committee, which carried on a campaign of consumer and worker education through posters, pamphlets, and the mass media. The information industry co-operated with metric articles and cartoons in newspapers and magazines and metric commercials on radio and television. The news media also started to use the metric system before the changeover date so that to keep abreast of affairs it was necessary to comprehend metrics. Today, it is estimated that 95 percent of the Japanese people understand the system and use it willingly.

There was some public opposition to the new system during the early years, particularly among oldsters, traditionalists, farmers, and fishermen, but on the whole the changeover in the public area went much more smoothly than had been anticipated. Early in the conversion some anonymous Japanese had the very good idea of inducing department stores in Tokyo to start selling candy by the gram instead of the momme—a unit of weight in the shaku-kan system. Kids who had learned about the gram in school accepted the change without a murmur—candy is desirable regardless of the system by which it is disbursed. The success of this experiment led to its extension to fish, meat, other produce, and yard goods. For a short time, housewives and shopkeepers experienced a little trouble in adapting to the new units, although youngsters were able to aid their parents in understanding the change.

Foodstuffs had usually been sold by the momme, the equivalent of 375 grams, and at first food was priced per 400 grams. This lost the benefits of the decimal system and was changed to pricing by 100 grams or kilograms. Complaints about the new policy disappeared in a surprisingly short time, and it is now not unusual for young people to have no concept of weights expressed in mommes or kans or lengths expressed in shakus or suns.

The building and real estate industries had some special problems in conversion. Residential construction practice in Japan has long been far in advance of the United States in terms of efficiency because Japanese houses are built on a pre-cut system based on standard modules. The modules were dimensioned in terms of the 2-inch-thick straw mats that form the floors of Japanese houses. These tatami mats were uniformly 6 shakus long and 3 shakus wide, as were the sliding doors with which rooms are divided. Room sizes are expressed in terms of so many mats—a 6-mat room, an 8-mat room, etc.

House sizes as well as land areas were expressed in "tsubo," an area equivalent to 2 tatami mats. Although land and buildings are now sold in terms of square meters, many people who can visualize a 50-tsubo building lot have some difficulty envisioning a land area of 165 square meters. Between 1960 and 1966, Japan completely rewrote all of the official records pertaining to the ownership of land to convert them to the metric system.

In manufacturing, Japan had one advantage in that much of its machinery was imported and thus represented a mixture of the metric and the Anglo-American systems. Many measuring instruments were calibrated in both millimeters and inches. The inch-based machinery was gradually modified when repair and overhaul became necessary, and tools graduated in both systems had the inch part obliterated. Worn-out and obsolete machinery based on the inch system is replaced with machines using the metric system.

One of the troublesome areas of conversion was in screw threads. The best standardized system for threaded fasteners is based on a certain number of threads to the inch. This Anglo-American system is generally recognized as superior to any metric standardization system that has yet been universally accepted, to the point that the International Organization for Standardization endorses both inch-based and metric standards for threader fasteners. Most Japanese factories that used Anglo-American screws are slowly shifting to metric fasteners.

The magazine *Measurements & Data* concluded a study of Japanese conversion with praise for the accomplishment:

> The conversion has proceeded smoothly within industry, receiving excellent cooperation from the business circles. There has been no demand for compensation by the government for large expenses incurred by industry in modifying their equipment. . . . International trade has been simplified, even though the United States, one of her major customers, is not on the metric system. The complete change from a mixed system of measurement to the disciplined, unified,

metric system has not injured Japan in any measurable way; on the contrary, it is believed that the simple relation between units for different quantities, which is the main advantage of the International System, is proving to be a boon for the country.

The metric conversion that is most meaningful to the United States is that which started in England in 1965. It is significant that the mother country of the Anglo-American system of weights and measures, from which America inherited her hodgepodge of units, has at long last decided that a foreign system will better serve her interests. England's decision to change was a rather sudden one and is indicative of the speed with which metric progress is isolating inch-pound countries. In a book published as recently as 1962 the author concluded, "The nations of the British Commonwealth, most of them eager to change to metric units a quarter-century ago, no longer consider the change feasible. The recent report of the special committee appointed by the Board of Trade in England advocated change, but the opposition it aroused was so sharp that the proposal may safely be considered dead." Three years later England decided to change.

Those who would belittle the significance of the British action as a bellwether for the United States point out that the principal factors underlying the British decision do not apply to the United States. A prime incentive for change was undoubtedly England's desire to become part of the European Common Market, which is fully metric. Also, British exports are approximately 15 percent of her total commerce, compared to some 5 percent for the United States; and most British exports are manufactured goods involving measured dimensions whereas only one-third of American exports are of this nature.

The difference here is only one of degree. England changed because she realized that her archaic and obsolete system was a handicap both politically and economically in a world that was becoming increasingly metricized. And, regardless of the *reason* for changing, the *problems* of conversion in the highly

industrialized island are comparable to those that the United
States would face. The only difference between the two countries is a psychological one. Preparation for England's change
to a decimal currency in 1971 conditioned the people to learning a new system; learning the metric system is merely another
step in a continuing procedure.

Metric opponents have always made much of the fact that
no country has ever converted to the system except under
government compulsion; that people had to be forced to accept something that they did not want. The change in England
nullifies that argument. The British government is advising
and cooperating, but the urge to convert came from private
business and industry.

Through the years, there have been periodic flare-ups of
controversy in England in connection with a change to the
metric system, as there have been in the United States. In
1951, a committee of the Board of Trade—a government
agency—studied the matter and reported that conversion to
the metric system was desirable but that it should only be
made in concert with the inch-pound countries with which
the United Kingdom traded. Nothing more was done until
1962, when the British Standards Institute, which is subsidized
by the government, sent out a questionnaire to industry that
disclosed that majority opinion recognized a change to the
metric system as inevitable and that it should be made forthwith, independent of action by the United States or members
of the Commonwealth.

This opinion was given more definite expression in February, 1965, in a letter from the Federation of British Industries—counterpart of America's National Association of
Manufacturers—to the President of the Board of Trade and
other government ministers. The letter commented on the
significant change in the outlook of British industry. "A majority both in numbers and total size . . . now favors the adoption of the metric system as the primary system of mensuration for British industry, as soon as that can be brought about
by general agreement." The letter concluded that the time

was "appropriate for a general statement of policy on the part of Her Majesty's Government, expressing support for the principle and giving some indication of the timing envisaged."

The government acted quickly. On May 24, 1965, in response to a question from the floor, the President of the Board of Trade read a statement to the House of Commons which is quoted in full because it clearly presents the position of the British government on conversion by free choice:

> The Government are impressed with the case which has been put to them by the representatives of industry for the metric system of weights and measures. Countries using that system now take more than one-half of our exports; and the total proportion of world trade conducted in terms of metric units will no doubt continue to increase. Against that background the Government consider it desirable that British industries on a broadening front should adopt metric units, sector by sector, until that system can become in time the primary system of weights and measures for the country as a whole.
>
> One necessary condition for advances in this field will be the provision of metric standards, wherever possible internationally recognized, which will enable particular sectors of industry to work in metric units. The Government have therefore asked the British Standards Institution—and the Institution have agreed—to pay special attention to this work and to press on with it as speedily as possible. The Government will, of course, take this new commitment into account in determining the amount of future grants-in-aid to the Institution. We are also considering how we can best encourage the educational work to familiarize future school generations and students in technological establishments with working in terms of metric units.
>
> We shall also encourage the change to the metric system as and when this becomes practicable for particular industries, by seeking to arrange that tenders for procurement by the Government and other public authorities shall be in terms of metric specifications.
>
> Practical difficulties attending the changeover will, of course, mean that this process must be gradual; but the

Government hope that within ten years the greater part of the country's industry will have effected the change. To this end they propose to establish a small standing joint committee of representatives of Government departments and industry to facilitate the removal of obstacles and to keep under constant review the progress which is being achieved.

The Government will keep in touch with Commonwealth Governments on this matter.

The British government proposes that the metric system shall become the *primary* system of weights and measures for the country; it is not contemplated that its use will be mandatory or that anybody will be fined or imprisoned for quaffing a pint of beer, quoting his weight in stones, or measuring a horse in hands. To date, no legislation has been passed on the subject and no compulsory legislation is contemplated. Existing laws governing weights and measures will have to be changed to convert Imperial to metric standards or to legalize new standards where merely converted standards are not convenient; for instance a speed limit of 30 miles an hour will certainly not become 48.28 kilometers an hour—the new limit will probably be 50 kilometers per hour.

The government will not subsidize any part of the cost of conversion because, says the British Standards Institute, "the long-term economic benefits will, it is suggested, more than balance the immediate outlay." There already exists what in England is called a "scheme" that provides a partial government subsidy for plant modernization under certain conditions, and metrication may qualify companies for such aid in some instances. Also, British tax law provides for a tax abatement for premature write-offs of equipment which would apply where machinery is replaced by metric equipment before the expiration of its normal depreciation period.

Initial participation of government in the conversion was threefold. It subsidized the British Standards Institute in preparing new metric standards in every area. It set up a Committee on Metrication with representatives of industry and government "to encourage, assist, and review the progressive adoption within British industry of the metric system of weights and measures." The committee co-ordinates government and industrial policies and makes recommendations to the Minister of Technology if it is generally agreed that more positive government action is required in any area. The committee also considers the implication of industrial changes in such areas as education, commerce, and government purchasing. Government is also responsible for directing the long-term program of education that is essential before any new system can be fully effective.

In 1969, four years after the decision to convert, the government established a Metrication Board, at the suggestion of the Metrication Committee, to act as a central planning agency and to be responsible for preparing the public for the change. The Minister of Technology described the new agency by saying,

> The Board will be advisory. The adoption of the metric system must be gradual, through democratic procedures based on the widest consultation. Membership of the Board will, therefore, reflect the interests of industry, the distributive trades, education—for which there are important implications—and, particularly, the general public and consumers. The Board will need to ensure that the distributive trades and consumers are consulted and have ample notice of proposed change. No compulsory powers will be sought. There can be no question of compensation; the costs of adopting metric weights must lie where they fall.

Without legal compulsion, government can exert much influence to insure industrial co-operation in the metrication program through its massive purchasing power. When the conversion program in each industry reaches a certain stage, the government will change its procurement procedures to express specifications in the metric system and require that products or construction covered by government contracts be built and packaged to metric specifications. A company that lags in metrication may find that it will be unable to do business with the government. The British Post Office has encouraged a change to metric standards for envelopes by charging extra postage for those that are smaller in dimensions than those of the International Organization for Standardization.

Although it is England's intention to convert to the metric system in all areas where weights and measures are used, the 10-year target date applies only to industrial conversion, since the primary purpose of the change is to create a better reception for British products in world markets. It is recognized that the metric system will ultimately have to be adopted universally, but changes in the retail area that will directly affect people as consumers will be a later operation.

England has wisely recognized that thorough planning is the key to making conversion as painless and economical as possible. For this they have adopted a technique, initially developed in the United States for aerospace projects, known as "critical path analysis." This technique enables each activity to be estimated in terms of the time needed for its completion and shows the interdependence of each co-related event. Key to the system is a chart known as P.E.R.T. (project evaluation and review technique) on which programming is portrayed to show each activity and reveal, if first estimates fail, which among the other activities will be affected in the general time scale.

The first step in the organization of conversion was to provide for changing to metric dimensions the fabricated raw materials and components used by industry. The change was planned so that the materials and components will arrive on time in relation to the programs of individual industries. Also, production rates for materials made to both new and old dimensions are planned for a smooth and economical transition. In the early stages of conversion, the old standards still prevail for most materials, and production by these standards will gradually decrease until only spare parts are being made for obsolescent equipment.

Before any materials can be fabricated or components produced to metric dimensions, standards must be accepted and agreed upon. Basically this involves a revision of stock sizes and quality, safety, and performance controls. During the first 5 years of the conversion period, the British Standards Institute revised about 1,400 basic standards, all that are necessary to enable industry to effect the changeover. Ultimately, a total of some 4,500 standards will have to be revised. Wherever possible, the new standards have been co-ordinated with those already recommended by the International Organization for Standardization. Converting standards is not merely a matter of changing existing ones to metric units on a purely mathematical basis. It would be pointless to convert a one-inch metal bar to its exact equivalent of 25.4mm when potential buyers of steel bars are using 25mm slots. In most cases, the new standards represent slightly different dimensions from those used under the inch system.

An important purpose of standards is to set a limitation on the number of sizes, shapes, or forms in which a material is fabricated. England has found that changing to metric standards offers an opportunity for a reduction in variety and a consequent saving in production costs. The old inch-pound standards did not grow from any preconceived plan. In many cases they developed piecemeal to meet particular demands, with the result that there was much duplication and unnecessary variety. For instance, one set of screw standards included 11 sizes in a given line. Nobody used all 11 sizes. It was found that some companies used only even-numbered sizes in their own specifications, while others used only odd-numbered sizes. The revised metric standards call for only 6 sizes.

A trade almanac of the paper industry showed 53 stock sizes. The International Organization for Standardization recommends an A series of papers in only 8 sizes. The largest size is AO, a sheet of one square meter with dimensions of 841 by 1189mm. Other standard sizes are arrived at by halving this sheet; A1 is a sheet 594 by 841mm, A2 420 by 594mm, and so forth down to A7. All stationery used for correspondence has been standardized to the A4 and A5 sizes. The creation of new standards presents a unique opportunity to rationalize stock size situations, and British industry has found that many out-of-date specifications and outmoded designs can be eliminated during the metrication process.

Conversion in manufacturing—as opposed to processing of materials—is taking place on an industry-by-industry basis. Each industry has developed its own program with a time-table that it considers most economical and efficient and which is co-ordinated with changes in materials and tools. Each program is considered by the Metrication Committee so that any action by government that may be necessary or advisable can be timed to fit the program. Dates are set for metric changes in specifications for government purchasing, for changes in education or training with which government is concerned, and for any revision of regulations that may be necessary.

The pharmaceutical industry was substantially converted before the program started, as it is in the United States. The paper making, printing, and publishing industries virtually completed their changeover in 1970 and the photographic industry expects to complete its conversion by 1972. The construction industry published its program in 1967. Since the beginning of 1969, designs for new projects have been in metric terms and, in 1970, conversion to the metric system in actual construction started; by the end of 1972 the changeover will have been substantially completed. The government has responded by setting January 1, 1972, as the date after which all bids for public building must be based on metric specifications. Since the government is financially involved in approximately 50 percent of all construction in England every company in the building industry has a strong inducement to convert by this date.

The program for the engineering industry was submitted in 1968 and provided a maximum planning period of two years, particularly on design and development. The big change in production—from 25 percent metric to 75 percent metric

—will take place between 1972 and 1975. Under the electrical industry program, which was adopted in 1969, the industry is split into 5 sectors, each having a different timetable. At one end of the scale is the production of accessories and components, which will convert to the metric system from 1971 to mid-1974; on the other end is power generation, transmission, and distribution equipment, in which most of the changeover will occur between 1972 and 1976. The main period of change for household electric appliances is from 1971 to the end of 1974. The electrical cable industry converted during 1970. The marine industry program, also adopted in 1969, provides for substantially complete conversion by the end of 1972.

Companies in the aircraft industry must keep a wary eye on the United States before making changes, because America is the prime customer for many of its products. The supersonic jet Concorde, which was jointly built by France and England, was made to a combination of inch-pound and metric specifications, with all drawings in both dimensions.

The automobile industry seems to be dragging its feet. Late in 1969 it stated, "The diversity of the industry, its manufacturing processes, suppliers and markets, pose a number of problems which make it impossible to predict a single changeover date. It is anticipated that many vehicle producers will use metric measurements and standards on vehicle model changes and when routine, major retooling becomes necessary." Here, too, the United States is the principal export customer. The Jaguar is already being built to metric specifications.

Although it may seem strange that a little thing like a screw should cause great conversion problems, any discussion of metrication inevitably turns to fasteners. During recent years, England has changed from two standardized systems, the Whitworth and the B.A., to another inch-based system that co-ordinates with the United States and Canada. Some opinion holds that fasteners should be left alone for a while; others feel that they should be the first thing tackled. The British

| **1** | Time taken to produce the programme |
|---|---|
| **2** | Preparatory studies |
| | **(a)** Time taken for BSI to produce its construction industry guide to the use of the metric system |
| | **(b)** Time required for BSI to produce key dimensional recommendations based on user studies |
| **3** | Essential reference publications |
| | **(a)** Time required to make available in metric terms essential reference publications of an *official* nature |
| | **(b)** Time required to make available in metric terms essential reference publications of an *industrial* nature |
| **4** | Products for which dimensional co-ordination is essential |
| | **(a)** Time required for manufacturers to provide technical information in metric terms for their products *as they are now produced* |
| | **(b)** Time required for BSI to produce metric dimensional recommendations and British Standards for these products |
| | **(c)** Time required for manufacturers to change to full production of new metric dimensionally-co-ordinated products |
| **5** | Products which are dimensionally related to those in Item 4 |
| | **(a)** Time required for manufacturers to provide technical information in metric terms for their products *as they are now produced* |
| | **(b)** Time required for BSI to produce metric dimensional recommendations and British Standards for these products |
| | **(c)** Time required for manufacturers to change to full production of new metric dimensionally-co-ordinated products |
| **6** | Products which are not dimensionally related to those in Item 4 |
| | **(a)** Time required for manufacturers to provide technical information in metric terms for their products *as they are now produced* |
| | **(b)** Time required for BSI to produce metric dimensional recommendations and British Standards for these products |
| | **(c)** Time required for manufacturers to change to full production of new metric dimensionally-co-ordinated products |
| **7** | Products which are only required to have sensible metric sizes and values |
| | **(a)** Time required for manufacturers to provide technical information in metric terms for their products *as they are now produced* |
| | **(b)** Time required for BSI to produce metric standards for these products |
| | **(c)** Time required for manufacturers to change to full production of their products to the new metric standards |
| **8** | Time required for manufacturers to produce all measuring instruments for the construction industry calibrated in metric terms |
| **9** | Time required for designers and quantity surveyors to change to the production of drawings and documents in metric terms *for all new contracts* |
| **10** | Time required for main contractors and sub-contractors to change to construction based on metric drawings and documents produced under Item 9 |

Date for the change to decimal
currency, February, 1971

| 1966 | 1967 | 1968 | 1969 | 1970 | 1971 | 1972 | 1973 | 1974 | |
|---|---|---|---|---|---|---|---|---|---|
| | Published February 1967 | | | | | | | | **1** |
| | | | | | | | | | **2** |
| | Published February 1967 | | | | | | | | (a) |
| | | | | | | | | | (b) |
| | | | | | | | | | **3** |
| | | | | | | | | | (a) |
| | | | | | | | | | (b) |
| | | | | | | | | | **4** |
| | | | | | | | | | (a) |
| | | | | | | | | | (b) |
| | | | | | | | | | (c) |
| | | | | | | | | | **5** |
| | | | | | | | | | (a) |
| | | | | | | | | | (b) |
| | | | | | | | | | (c) |
| | | | | | | | | | **6** |
| | | | | | | | | | (a) |
| | | | | | | | | | (b) |
| | | | | | | | | | (c) |
| | | | | | | | | | **7** |
| | | | | | | | | | (a) |
| | | | | | | | | | (b) |
| | | | | | | | | | (c) |
| | | | | | | | | | **8** |
| | | | | | | | | | **9** |
| | | | | | | | | | **10** |

This vertical bar shows the date by which the
change to metric should be effectively complete.

KEY

Period for preliminary preparations

Period during which the bulk of
the change will be taking place

Period during which residual
changes will probably continue

Standards Institute has taken the position that, "it is strongly recommended that British industry should adopt the International Standards Organization Metric Screw Thread System."

The program for each industry is portrayed on a chart that shows the timing of the several steps. The chart for the building industry, which portrays its program in 10 separate steps with a timetable for each, is reproduced on the preceding 2 pages. The first 2 steps, the production of the program and preparatory studies, were completed in 1966. Under Step 3, reference publications were revised from 1966 to 1968. Steps 4 to 7 deal with the conversion of building products, and each of these steps is divided into 3 sections: the time required to prepare metric information, the time required to determine standards, and the time required to produce.

Building construction, in England as in the United States, has been essentially a craft-based industry in which things are made to fit with one another by altering their size or shape on the site. Architects and construction engineers have long had a keen desire to replace this archaic system with a more rational approach to building involving more widespread use of standardized dimensions for building products and elements. The British construction industry has taken advantage of metrication to accomplish this by changing dimensions not only to sensible metric sizes but to ones that can be coordinated and assembled on the job with a minimum of labor. The application of this system varies for different elements, hence the 4 separate planning and timing steps. Step 4 covers products for which full dimensional co-ordination is desirable, including such things as structural panels, window units, kitchen fittings, and appliances. Other products, such as bricks, wall coverings, and sheet materials must be dimensionally related to those in the first group; these are in Step 5. Those in Step 6, which include heating and air-conditioning equipment, need not be dimensionally related to other products. The group in Step 7—door hardware, paint, nails, glass, etc.—need only have sensible metric sizes.

Step 8, which covers changes in measuring instruments for

the industry, was, for the most part, completed during 1968–69. Much of this merely involved the application of overlay dials. Step 9 covers the time required for designers and surveyors to change to the production of drawings and documents in metric terms. Step 10 covers the period for actual change to metric construction.

The program for the engineering industry is in some ways simpler and in other ways more complex than that of the construction industry. Basic metric standards were created in this industry in 1968 and 1969. The main period of conversion to metric materials, tools, and components is from 1971 to 1974. Most metric design and development is scheduled for 1970–1973. Major production planning using metric materials and designs will range from 1970 to 1974. The principal period of change to metric production will be 1972 to 1975.

To date, conversion in the British engineering industry indicates that many, if not most, of the claims made by metric opponents in the United States regarding cost and confusion are extremely unrealistic. Costs are inversely related to the time allowed; those companies that make an early start can expect to make the changeover more economically than those who delay. The engineering program does not call for crash conversion that would immediately make obsolete all existing tools, machines, and models. "In general," it says, "it will only be possible to introduce completely metric designs at approximately the normal rate of introduction of new designs. Redesigning in metric terms will generally be considered only when commercial reasons dictate a new design, either to take advantage of technological improvements or because the profitability of the product has declined." Some day in the future, the difficulty of obtaining inch-dimensioned materials and tools will influence redesign of products that might not otherwise be changed.

Industries whose products do not have to co-ordinate with other products and are sold only in the domestic market may not change for many years; and, in a few cases, things are made to inch-pound standards all over the world and will continue to be so made in the forseeable future. In such cases, metrication merely involves dual dimensioning on drawings. Frequently, the most expensive type of metrication is associated with internal parts, the size and shape of which are of no concern to the customer. Partial metrication may make such products compatible with a metric environment—redesigning only exterior dimensions and using metric hardware items which are most subject to replacement. An electric motor is a good example of this type of product.

Much has been made of the tremendous cost of replacing inch-based machine tools. Say the British, "The general experience of those who have already embarked upon metric production is that in very few cases indeed will machine tools require complete replacement, but some may require modification. . . . Work has been completed on devices which will enable machine indices to read in hundredths of millimeters instead of, or as well as, thousandths of an inch." It has also been learned that a majority of inch-based cutting and measuring equipment can be used for metric production, although this is recommended only during a transition period or until such tools are normally replaced. A comparison of tables of drill diameters discloses that, in some cases, inch-dimensioned drills may be used to produce holes within the tolerances of metric specifications.

Planning for the program brought to light some problems that would seem to be minor but that are not as inconsequential as they appear at first glance. There seems to be no way to avoid a double inventory of materials, components, and tools during the transition period, and duplicate storage space is necessary. However, it was found that storage space is more closely related to the range of items stored than to their quantity, and the reduction in variety that new standards may bring about will offset the duplication and ultimately result in a saving of storage space.

Identification is another problem that may not be as minor as it seems. If metric parts and inch parts are both used during a transition period, how does the worker tell them apart? An automobile assembly line is a good example of this. On present assembly lines, different models are mixed on the same line but many of the parts used are the same—both a convertible and a sedan use one-half-inch screws. But if some models used metric screws and others inch screws a system would have to be devised to prevent workers from putting the wrong screw in the wrong model. Color coding seems to be the obvious answer, but many parts are already color coded to denote such things as antirust treatment—and some workers are color-blind. No overall solution to this problem has yet been proposed.

Another international difficulty that England's conversion creates is the means of denoting a decimal point. In England, as in the United States, this is done by a period. In most metric countries a comma is used—5,750 would not be read as five thousand seven hundred and fifty but as five and seven hundred and fifty thousandths. It is hoped that the period can be made universal as the decimal point and, until this is done, that a space be substituted for the comma in groups of numbers having more than three digits; thus 5 750. The financial fraternity objects to this on the grounds that the space would provide opportunity for the fraudulent insertion of an extra figure.

To symbolize the metric changeover, the British Standards Institute has designed this Metric Symbol Key that companies that have converted may use in their advertising, catalogs,

# Outline network analysis of the introduction of a metric product

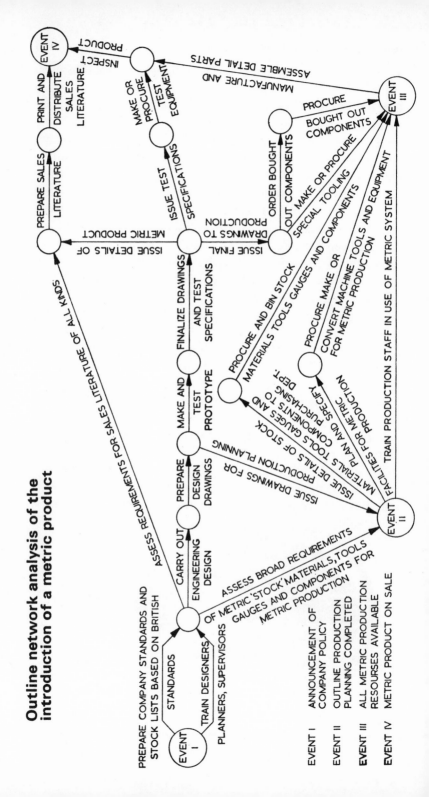

EVENT I — ANNOUNCEMENT OF COMPANY POLICY

EVENT II — OUTLINE PRODUCTION PLANNING COMPLETED

EVENT III — ALL METRIC PRODUCTION RESOURCES AVAILABLE

EVENT IV — METRIC PRODUCT ON SALE

and on metric products. The Institute emphasizes that it must not be used on imported metric goods, as its purpose is to mark metric goods made in the United Kingdom.

Although each individual company will have some unique problems in conversion, there is a certain overall pattern to the process that applies to all companies. A chart prepared by the British Standards Institute portraying this pattern in four "events" is reproduced here.

Pending changes in education that will familiarize personnel with the metric system, industry faces the need to retrain present workers. This must be timed to key in with other aspects of the changeover. Obviously, there is no point in giving a man a metric tool until he has learned to use it; on the other hand, if training is started too early a worker may have to be retrained when the time comes to apply his new knowledge.

The extent of training that is necessary depends on the individual job. Although it is possible that filing clerks or floor sweepers could continue to do their work with no knowledge of the metric system, most personnel will need some training. Engineers and high-level technicians will have to learn the system thoroughly; a stock room clerk need know only the metric nomenclature for the material that he dispenses. It has been found that those who need to know the most are usually the easiest to train. Those in advanced technical jobs have both the interest and the intellectual capacity virtually to train themselves, whereas the machine operator who knows, or thinks that he knows, how big a "thou" of an inch is may find it very difficult to accept measurements in hundredths of a millimeter. Conversion progress to date discloses that most workers can cope with the change if they are given reasonable time. "In fact," says an official of the British Standards Institute, "we may have tended to overestimate the amount of training needed for operators."

To introduce the metric system to all workers, the government has issued plant posters and leaflets showing the basic units of the system, including one popular poster showing a pretty girl in a bikini with her hip, waist, and bust measurements marked in centimeters. Industries that have started to convert have prepared conversion charts for various operations showing inch-pound and metric equivalents. All training experts agree that these should be used as sparingly as possible, for the important part of training is to induce the worker to "think metric." Workers must not only be taught the system; they must be induced to accept it.

To accomplish this, most companies are using an "associability" technique, which puts employees in a metric environment where familiar things are expressed in metric dimensions. Some have painted metric measurements on the floors of plants and offices and on door jambs. Some use associability charts or displays on which familiar objects marked with metric dimensions are displayed. A soccer ball is labeled "250mm diameter," a 5-gallon can is marked "about 20 litres", a pint beer mug is labeled "approximately one-half litre." It is important in this technique that the objects portrayed be standard items with which the worker has long been familiar; a new half-litre container instead of a pint beer mug would not serve the purpose of associability. Also, no inch or pound measurements are shown; the purpose is to get the worker to think metric, not to convert.

Those who make much of the cost of conversion ignore the opportunities for profit by entrepreneurs who offer new goods or services that will expedite the process. Typical is a company that styles itself "Instant Metrics, Ltd." and advertises, "Instant metric system installed in your works by our engineers; instantly converts existing inch machines to dual-measuring systems." Other companies are producing pocket sliding scales showing conversion from metric to Imperial and vice versa. One enterprise publishes an industrial training system for the building industry called Metripack. This consists of thirty lessons, or modules, each complete in itself but together covering the whole range of metric knowledge required by anyone in the industry. Companies that buy the system list their personnel by job descriptions and each employee takes a simple adaptive test from which is determined the individual training required. Metripack then supplies the specific modules for each employee that will give him the training that he needs for his job.

A visitor to England 5 years after the decision to convert finds nothing, or virtually nothing, changed. In fact, England's decision to go metric seems to have been received more dramatically in the United States than at home. All that is going on behind the scenes is not evident to the casual observer. The reaction of individual British companies to the change is said to vary from passive acceptance to enthusiastic opportunism. Business and technical societies are delighted that meetings at which metrication is discussed are attended by overflow audiences. Such opposition as there was when the decision was made has virtually ceased. "All concerned now seem keen to get on with the job and get it over."

There are still a few die-hards. An organization calling itself the British Measures Research Group bombards business executives and members of Parliament with letters saying:

> In the interests of democracy we draw attention to the underhand methods on a national scale involving the changeover to metrics now being sponsored by Government Departments and quasi-Government bodies. This is a matter of the greatest importance that will permanently affect every British citizen. Yet going metric has never been discussed in Parliament nor authorized there.

This group obviously does not keep pace with Parliamentary debates. One crusty conservative in the House of Lords repeatedly makes speeches bemoaning the loss of the beloved and traditional Imperial system and demanding that the changeover be stopped. The Federation of Building Trades Employees insists that metrication will increase the cost of homes and demands that the government do something about it. Naturally, the labor unions in the building industry do not like a change that will ultimately decrease on-the-site labor.

The Secretary of the Metrication Committee summarized

the program and the progress of industrial conversion 2 years after it started as follows:

> And so the small rivulets come together to make a stream, and later a river. The situation does not call for a new ukase, like Magna Carta's "one measure of wine shall be used throughout our Kingdom, and one measure of ale, and one measure of corn, to wit, the London quarter"—presumably the first Standard in Britain. It is a long haul; and the biggest haul has to be made by industry itself, at varying pace. . . . But . . . one thing seems to me to be sure; and that is that the momentum has gathered pace in the last twelve months, and that the rivulets will become fast flowing rivers much more quickly than one would have believed even one year ago.

There has been much controversy about metrication in the public area. For a time, the Board of Trade maintained that British industry could go metric while the retail sector stayed with Imperial measures. The Ministry of Technology held a contrary view that finally prevailed, and the government is committed to a policy of complete metrication, although no target date other than that for industry has been set. The Metrication Board has recommended that the government announce 1975 as the desirable date for retail as well as industrial conversion.

There is considerable difference of opinion as to when the public program should begin. The Federation of British Industries has been campaigning for an early start, claiming that unless the retail sector adopts the metric system simultaneously with industrial conversion, some manufacturers would have to make metric products for export and inch products for home consumption. The British Standards Institute recommends that public conversion should be coincidental with the change to decimal currency, the date for which is February 15, 1971. The Consumers Council disagrees, saying "the magnitude of a simultaneous change would be too great for consumers to cope with." The Council proposes that the change in the retail sector start some time after February, 1971, with the hope of completion by 1975.

All of this discussion is somewhat irrelevant; it is very unlikely that most Britons will be buying their beer in half-liters and their butter in half-kilos by 1975 because much new legislation is required before the change can take place. The Weights and Measures Act of 1963 specifies 57 foodstuffs, ranging from blanc-mange powder to vodka, that must be sold in prescribed Imperial quantities if they are prepackaged; 40 non-foodstuffs are covered by a similar regulation. The law permits exact metric conversion in packaging; a pound of butter could be marked "453.6 grams," but it would not be legal to package butter in half-kilo units of 500 grams. There are many other laws, by-laws, and regulations specifying Imperial measurements that will have to be changed before packaging in sensible metric sizes becomes legal in all areas of public use. An overall P.E.R.T. chart contemplates a 6-year period of conversion in this section of the economy that rules out a 1975 date for completion even if the necessary legislation was enacted immediately. One opinion concludes that "it will be many years before the inch and the pound join the fotmal and the chauldron as museum curiosities."

Ultimately, the metric system will have to become universal, or almost universal, for several basic reasons. When industry is completely converted, people will have to understand the metric system to hold a job, and it is inconceivable that schools would permanently teach the arithmetic necessary to use two separate systems, or that industry would maintain special training courses. Manufacturers of products used in both industry and the home will not make separate lines for each market; a screw manufacturer who is making the bulk of his product to metric standards for industrial use is not going to make a few inch screws to sell in hardware stores. Also, some products that may not in themselves require metrication except for export will have to be co-ordinated with things that are metrified. Kitchen work surfaces have been 36 inches high; after 1972 they will be 90cm, about one-half inch lower. A dishwasher built to go under a 36-inch shelf will not go under a 90cm shelf, nor will a 36-inch range be level with it.

With industry at the halfway mark in the conversion program in point of time, the British public has, on the whole, taken no interest in the matter. They are concerned only with the change to decimal currency on Feb. 15, 1971, which wipes out the 240-penny pound. The pound remains but equals 100 new cents, called pennies. The halfpenny has already gone the way of the farthing and will soon be followed by the shilling, the florin, and the half-crown. Decimal coins include a new halfpenny, worth 1.2¢ in American money; a penny, equal to 2.4¢; a 5-penny piece, equal to the old shilling, or 12¢; a 10-penny piece, which equals a florin, or 24¢; and a 50-penny piece, worth half a pound or $1.20.

One correspondent writes from London:

> As for the coming metric system, I don't think many people are aware of what it is going to entail. Most have no idea that feet and inches etc. are going to disappear; some admit that they have heard something about it but have forgotten exactly what. My impression is that we, who are creatures that tend to cling to tradition, will oppose it and make a fuss and try to pretend that we don't understand it, and thus show our loyalty to the old system and our suspicion of anything new. After this, I think, we will then realize that metrication is going to affect us quite a lot and will adapt to it. But as yet most of us do not fully realize what is going to happen in a few years time.

Most of the limited press comment on public metrication has been of a humorous nature, such as a cartoon showing a tailor measuring a man for a suit and saying, "I feel we should prepare ourselves for being 121.92 round the seat when we go metric, sir." There was a rash of humorous comment when the maternity section of a hospital in Ipswich started to quote babies' birth statistics in metric terms—weight 3.5k, length 53cm for a 7-pound 10-ounce baby 21 inches long. There have been several jokes about new measurements for shapely females; nobody can envision a girl whose statistics are 90-62-90—centimeters, that is. One columnist bemoans the passage of the poetry of apothecaries' scruples and drams and maintains that he cannot bear to see the passing of the hoppus foot—a unit which was used for centuries to measure trees and which some eager statistician has figured as equalling 0.036054 cubic meter. If the experience of flower growers on the Scilly Islands is any indication, there may be much latent resentment against the new system. They tried to market their blooms in bunches of 10 but had to go back to a dozen because, said one, "Our customers made it very clear that they want twelves and they will jolly well have twelves."

On the other hand, a small experiment that was made by members of the British Standards Institute in a shopping center on the outskirts of Sheffield indicated that people were interested, co-operative, and adapted quite readily to both decimal currency and metrication without much trouble. During the experiment, a bank set up counters in the stores to change old currency to plastic replicas of new coins and everything was priced in decimal currency and measured in metric units. Bananas were 15¢ a kilo, candy 5¢ per 100 grams, beer was sold in the local pub at 5¢ for the metric equivalent of one-half pint. Business was so good that the bank ran out of phoney money. Said one of the sponsors, "If the problems that arise to the man and woman in the street are no greater than those that appeared to exist in this experiment we shall at modest cost in temporary inconvenience have gained enormously by making it easier for ourselves to trade with the rest of the world and by reducing still further the disadvantage to our children of having to learn an archaic system."

Despite the lack of concrete planning there has been much high-level speculation concerning retail conversion. It is obvious that it will be a long process and that the extent of metrication may vary widely in different fields. Some areas of retailing may stay on the Imperial system until a generation of customers that does not understand it grows up. Greengrocers, whose products are not prepackaged in England to the same extent that they are in the United States, may continue to use pounds and ounces indefinitely. This is a self-contained trade in which little exporting is involved. Cook books have long lives and although metric cook books will be published their early sales will probably be limited to the relatively few people who like innovations. Kitchen measurements will undoubtedly remain largely in the Imperial system for many years. What will happen to ready-made clothing is anybody's guess. Items that are sized by body measurements may change when it becomes commonplace to consider such measurements in the metric system—a size 16 shirt in England is size 41 on the Continent; a size 7 hat, which denotes the diameter of the head in inches, is size 57 in metric measure—the circumference of the head in centimeters. Garments that are sold by size codings, such as some lines of women's dresses, may not change, although metrication would present an opportunity for the garment industry to adopt one standard sizing system. The British shoe industry is already working on an international metric sizing system for footwear to replace the ancient practice of basing shoe sizes on barleycorns.

In some fields, metric dimensioning will have little meaning to consumers; whether a sofa or a sideboard is 6'6" or 2 m long is of no concern to the buyer so long as it fits the wall space available. In other areas, complete metrication will not come until present measuring devices are normally replaced. Meters now measure gas by the cubic foot and electricity by the kilowatt-hour. Under the metric system, both gas and electricity would be priced by the joule but it would be a rather simple matter for utility companies to convert meter readings to joules and merely bill by the new system until the old meters wear out. With metric pricing, users can directly compare the heat output of gas and electric appliances.

Prepackaged foodstuffs create the greatest problem in conversion, if only because this is the area in which consumers most frequently come up against measurements. Simple mathematical conversion from Imperial units will seldom be satisfactory because it would involve odd metric measurements; approximately 453 grams instead of a pound or 1.08 liters instead of an Imperial quart. The Consumer Council has published a few new units that will probably be used.

| PRODUCT | IMPERIAL MEASURE | APPROXIMATE METRIC EQUIVALENT | POSSIBLE METRIC AMOUNT |
|---|---|---|---|
| Jam | 1 lb. | 453 g | 500 g |
| Beer | 1 pt. | 0.59 l | 0.50 l |
| Potatoes | 5 lbs. | 2.27 kg | 3 kg |
| Butter | ½ lb. | 227 g | 250 g |
| Tea | ¼ lb. | 114 g | 125 g |
| Whisky (tot) | 1/6 gill | 24 ml | 25 or 30 ml |

Some food packers are already marking containers with dual measurements, giving the exact metric conversion of the Imperial contents. Most informed opinion considers that this practice does little to acquaint people with the metric system and to get them to "think metric." Since England officially adopted the Celsius system for temperature in 1962 weather information has been reported in both this system and Fahrenheit units. After 8 years, virtually nobody knows whether 30° C. foretells a heat wave or a snow storm; they listen to the familiar Fahrenheit reading and mentally "switch off" for the Celsius.

Changes to metric sizes in some food packaging will be complicated and costly. It is relatively simple to adjust most packaging machines to deliver 500 grams instead of a pound and to increase the price proportionately by 10 percent. But the change will necessitate new dimensions for containers, new dimensions for the cartons in which units are shipped, new sizes for pallets on which cartons are transported and stored, and new dimensions for truck bodies to use shipping space efficiently.

In some cases, there may be a bright side to the change. The pint is the most popular size for milk containers in England—

Britons do not drink as much milk as Americans. The logical change would be a half-liter bottle, about 90 percent of a pint (the Imperial pint is more than one-half liter, the United States pint less than one-half liter). In half-liter containers the dairy industry would have to handle more bottles to sell the same amount of milk or, as would probably happen, people would use less milk. The National Dairymen's Association is considering switching to a 600ml bottle containing 5½ percent more than a pint in the hope that people will buy the same number of bottles and therefore use more milk. They could continue to use present crates and bottling equipment by merely raising the shoulder of the pint bottle.

In the south of England, where a drink of whisky is commonly a sixth of a gill—24ml—the liquor industry would benefit if the unit changed to 25ml and would profit handsomely from a change to 30ml, although the consequent difference in price may cause some heated arguments in bars. One thing is certain; the Englishman is going to continue to call his glass of beer a pint or half-pint whether it is measured in pints or liters.

The situation in British schools, as in the retail area, is somewhat muddled. The Schools Council issued the following statement: "It is for teachers to decide, on the basis of their own knowledge of their own children, whether, until nearer the time for the introduction of metric measures, the extension to metrication is desirable." The Royal Society took issue with this. At a meeting in 1968 attended by representatives of all elements of education it passed a resolution "that in primary schools there should be a change of emphasis in favor of the metric system of weights and measures from September 1969."

The schools are the key to complete metrication. Few adults who have lived with the inch-pound system all their lives will ever completely learn to "think metric." But children who are introduced to metrics as the primary or only system will never learn to think Imperial. Educators know that they must radically revise curriculum in this area but, in England as in the United States, they are a conservative group and do not hold with making changes quickly. When examining boards announced their intention of using metric questions in some examinations by 1970 an indignant letter to *The Times* from the head of a mathematics department protested such precipitate action, saying, "We must have at least two years' notice."

Aside from the attitude of teachers and educational administrators, there are some practical problems. New text books must be published and money provided to buy them. Before they are published they must be written, and for this there must be some agreement on how much metric and how much Imperial teaching they should contain and how the metric system should be presented. There is already some confusion. One educational supplier offers a set of metric capacity measures marked 125cc, 250cc, 500cc, and one liter; another produces measures in units of a centiliter, deciliter, half-liter, and liter. It will be a number of years before practice becomes unified.

Although government insists that no compulsion will be used, educational agencies associated with government have taken steps that will require early, positive action by schools to give the metric system more prominence in the curriculum. England has 14 regional Examination Boards that set standards for tests that students must pass to obtain certifications of accomplishment at various levels. A few of these boards have not yet taken a firm position as to when metric units will be used in examination questions. One says, "The Board is not prepared to commit itself absolutely to complete metrication by any particular date." However, most boards have set dates starting from 1969 to 1971 and requiring complete conversion at various times from 1972 to 1975. One board says, "The Board has decided to introduce metrication slowly from 1971." Another states, "The S.I. system of metric units will be adopted for use not later than the 1972 examinations." The Oxford and Cambridge Schools Examination Board states, "The Board would like to use the S.I. system exclusively in the examinations of 1972 and thereafter, with the following exceptions: [the exceptions include Domestic Science, Handicrafts, and Economics; in these both systems will be used]." Obviously, schools must make early provision to prepare children for Board Examinations on which questions are expressed in metric units.

Undaunted by the absence of equipment, some progressive teachers in the lower primary grades have licked the problem by having the children make their own equipment: cardboard meter sticks divided into decimeters and centimeters and cardboard metric squares and cubes. The reports on this experimental work are uniformly favorable. Kids have a fine time measuring sand, water, and the lengths of familiar objects with their metric equipment. Those in the lower grades, who have never been exposed to formal teaching of the Imperial system, accept metric measurements as a matter of course.

In secondary schools, students are already using metric units in those subjects that relate to future jobs, particularly in scientific, technical, and engineering courses. By the time these youngsters graduate, such knowledge will be essential in their work world but not in the daily world. Some high schools are taking a first step in familiarizing girls with the system that they will some day have to face as homemakers by introducing metric units in home economics courses on marketing, dressmaking, and cooking and nutrition. If any enterprising reader would like to make some cheese scones by the metric system, here is a recipe being used in a high school in Scotland: There are approximately 28 grams to an avoirdupois ounce.

| Imperial | Metric |
|---|---|
| 8 oz. flour | 250g self-rising flour* |
| 1 teaspoon baking powder | 30g margarine |
| | 60g grated cheese |
| 1 oz. margarine | ¼ teaspoon salt |
| 2 oz. grated cheese | pinch cayenne pepper |

¼ teaspoon salt
pinch cayenne pepper
¼ pint milk
Bake in hot oven (425°
F.) for 10–12 minutes.

150–175 ml milk
Bake in hot oven (230°
C.) for 10–12 minutes

* Self-rising flour was used to avoid the problem of the inaccuracy of the teaspoonful in relation to grams of flour.

The problem of the educators is compounded by the lack of decision on a program of conversion in the public area. So long as Imperial units are extensively used in retailing, the schools must teach them together with metric units, but it is certain that children who are now entering school will graduate into a metric world for which they must be prepared. The Schools Council expresses it thus:

> Although it is industry which is now in the process of changing over (and all indications are that the change will have been substantially completed by 1975) there is no doubt that the country as a whole is now firmly set on the metric road and eventually all our measurements in factories, shops, offices, and at home will be conducted in metric terms. The only issues still to be debated are those of timing, and although no one supposes that Imperial units will disappear completely in the next decade or so, we must at least work on the assumption that the generation now entering the schools will emerge into a world where the metric system will be dominant and familiarity with its use an indispensable qualification at work as well as in the home.

As of the end of the 1960's, several other countries were in the early stages of conversion or had decided to undertake the change. In 1968, the Irish government issued a statement saying, "The Government would expect that the greater part of Irish industry will have converted to the metric system by 1975." In the same year, the African countries of Kenya, Tanzania, and Uganda announced that metric units would become compulsory on January 1, 1969, and that thereafter nonmetric imports would be delayed and subject to penalties. The Government of Rhodesia announced its intention to convert in 1969.

In 1968, a committee of the Australian Senate recommended "that the use of Imperial units of measurement be discontinued over a period of time and that at the end of that period the metric system of units become the sole Commonwealth legal units of measurement." The Minister of Industries and Commerce of New Zealand announced that "conversion to the metric system is a logical step for New Zealand. . . . The Government accepts the necessity of assisting metrication in New Zealand."

For many years, American opponents of the metric system have made much of the fact that all English speaking nations, who had always led the way in industrial, commercial, and technological progress, were unified in their adherence to the inch-pound system. Today there is no English speaking bloc in opposition to the rest of the world. The United States and Canada stand alone in support of what cannot even be called an American system, since all of the other countries in the Americas have converted to the metric system.

# 7

# WHERE WE
# STAND TODAY

After more than a century and a half of argument, it is virtually certain that the great metric controversy will be resolved for the United States during the current decade. Indirectly, Russia was responsible for setting afoot the trend of events that will lead to a settlement.

When the Russians first orbited the earth with Sputnik I in 1957 it became apparent that they were well ahead of the United States in the race for space. Partially responsible for this was the fact that they had discarded their outmoded system of measurements 30 years before; had they not converted to the metric system they could not have launched their first satellite so soon after World War II ended.

Stirred to action by the realization that the Communists were well out in front, the United States established the National Aeronautics and Space Administration to conduct and co-ordinate nonmilitary research on problems of space flight. The 15,000 scientists, engineers, and technicians at NASA work almost exclusively in the metric system, although their findings have to be converted to inch-pound units for production of most space hardware. To maintain liaison between NASA and the Congress, the House of Representatives established in 1958 a Committee on Science and Astronautics. One of several things for which this committee was made responsible is a consideration of the metric system.

147

Congressman Charles Miller of California became chairman of the committee in 1961. He immediately proposed a bill to provide for a 3-year study of the metric system by the Department of Commerce. This bill ran into difficulties in the House Rules Committee and never reached the floor; the aged chairman of the Rules Committee is alleged to have asked, "What is this *meet-ric* system?" Congressman Miller reintroduced a similar bill in 1963 and Senator Claiborne Pell of Rhode Island offered a companion bill in the Senate in the same year. Finally, in August of 1968, the Miller-Pell bills were passed and became Public Law 90-472, which provides for the first full-scale investigation of the country's weights and measures since John Quincy Adams made his study in 1817.

The law authorizes the Secretary of Commerce

> . . . to conduct a program of investigation, research and survey to determine the impact of increasing worldwide use of the Metric System on the United States; to appraise the desirability and practicability of increasing the use of metric weights and measures in the United States; to study the feasibility of retaining and promoting the international use of dimensional and other engineering standards based on the Customary measurements of the United States; and to evaluate the costs and benefits of alternative courses of action which may be feasible for the United States.

The project is being handled by a Metric System Study Group in the Bureau of Standards. It is estimated that it will take 3 years and cost $2,500,000.

Hopefully, the Metric Study Group will conduct its work in a less emotional setting than that which prevailed at past Congressional hearings, and the biggest headlines will not be made by prophets of doom who predict utter chaos from conversion. Although the law covering the activity specifies that the study should embrace educational, engineering, manufacturing, commercial, public, and scientific areas, it is obvious that primary attention will be focused on the impact of the

change to industry. Of the 43 members of the panel from outside government that has been set up to advise on the study,
30 members represent industry or labor. The consumer is represented by but one member of the panel, as are education,
retail trade, agriculture, communications, real estate, sports,
and advertising. Additional advisors in some or all of these
areas may be added to the panel as time goes on.

A concern for the world position of the United States politically as well as economically undoubtedly influenced Congress
to take long overdue action that will probably lay the ground-
work for adoption of the metric system. With the conversion
of England, which will be followed by other Commonwealth
countries, the United States stands alone (except for a few inconsequential allies) in an all-metric world. America has spent
many billions of dollars during the past quarter century to
build a firm foundation for a free world; it has taken the
leadership in creating alliances in both Europe and the Pacific
to this end. With the switch of other English speaking countries to the metric system, the United States and, possibly,
Canada will be the *only* members of NATO or SEATO to use
another system. The United States led in the establishment
of the Pan American Union, which endorsed the metric system at its first meeting. Today, the United States is the only
member of the Union that does not use this system.

Dr. Edward Teller, father of the hydrogen bomb, described
America's situation as follows:

> Our nation has embarked on one of the most tremendous
> and inspiring, but dangerous, enterprises in history; we have
> set out to build an industrialized and lawful world free from
> war and free from economic misery. We are now so involved
> in this undertaking that unless we succeed we may cease to
> exist. The danger of being overtaken by Russia in our
> accelerating contest for world leadership is very real. In this
> important contest it seems inconceivable that we should
> allow ourselves to be hamstrung by a situation which has
> hurt us in the past, is hurting us today, and will continue to
> hurt us in the future. But the fact is that the United States

is out of step with the rest of the world in an immensely significant way: we measure things differently.

Adherence to the inch-pound system is handicapping the United States in its conflict with Communism around the world. The extent of this burden cannot be defined, but it is certainly an advantage to the Communist countries that their engineers, businessmen, and diplomats talk the same measurement language as the rest of the world. The United States and Russia are vying for the good will of nations that are seeking to industrialize or that have recently emerged from colonialism. All of these nations use the same system as Russia. When the United States, at great expense, provides technical assistance in Latin America, Africa, or India, the people whom they are helping do not understand a very important element of what the Americans are trying to teach; before communication can be established they have to learn the inch-pound system or the teachers have to learn the metric system. Communist engineers and technicians have no such handicap in dealing with underdeveloped countries.

Despite the imminent isolation of the United States in an all-metric world the controversy is by no means dead. In recent years, it has become somewhat more moderate in tone, on the whole, although there are still radicals on both sides who predict dire consequences if we convert or economic strangulation if we do not. One metric proponent writes, "Unless we act *now,* about the year 2000 we will experience a depression that will make the 30's look like a Sunday School picnic." He is answered by a chorus of antimetrics who claim that the cost of conversion would be so staggering that it would wreck the economy of the country.

Antimetrics were still repeating, in the 1960's, many of the objections to the system that they used in the early part of the century. In a recent letter to *Science,* Joseph Mayer, an ardent metric critic who headed up the National Industrial Conference Board study in 1921, reiterates that "It is just about as sensible to attempt to substitute the metric for

WHERE WE STAND TODAY

the English system in the United States as it would be to substitute the French for the English language." He repeats that
only one-tenth of one percent of the people would benefit by
the use of the metric system and still insists that a great fault
of this system is that it is not scientific. "The recent adoption
of a wavelength of light as an invariable standard for the
international unit of length has broken the propaganda line
that the meter is more fundamental than the inch and has
shattered the illusion that the metric system is in any sense
scientific, immutable or sacrosanct." Mayer's views are those
of a group of antimetrics who propose that the inch-pound
system be standardized, streamlined, and simplified—principally by increased decimalization—so that the "internationally
recognized English system will continue to stand forth not
only as a worthy competitor for world-wide recognition but
also as largely superior to metricism in covering the many
uses which a really comprehensive, flexible, common, and
handy system of weights and measures must embrace."

The chauvinists are still a noisy factor in the controversy,
with their insistence that the American way is the best way
and that we must cling to it regardless of what others do. Although the argument that the metric system is sacrilegious is
no longer heard, there are still those who maintain that it is
unpatriotic. The inch and the pound are, in their view, sacred
American traditions; to tamper with them would be to un-
dermine American principles of freedom and liberty.

The chauvinists intimate that those who advocate adoption
of the metric system serve foreign interests. Typical of this
view is an article in the *Naval Engineers Journal* in which the
author recommends that "the ethnic origin of every advocate
of the metric system be meticulously examined and evaluated
in terms of reference to the overall welfare of the USA now
and in the future." In this writer's opinion, those metric advocates who are not impractical eggheads are probably anti-
American subversives. Another aspect of this thinking is that
the United States should maintain its traditional system as a
"secret weapon" in foreign relations; in this view, the fact

that others do not understand it gives us an advantage. Conversely, Nobel prize winner Harold Urey has called the metric system "a secret weapon of Communism."

Isolationism, which became a dirty word after World War II in most areas of American affairs, still prevails in the metric controversy. Some of this is based on pure chauvinism, but there is a basis for it that is at least partially defensible in terms of measurement standards. The consideration of measurement systems is a separate issue from the question of standardization, but the two are intimately intertwined. A universal measuring system is rather meaningless without universal standards, and adopting a universal system would be a form of standardization.

The concept of standardization in industrial production was born in the United States. Eli Whitney, famed for his cotton gin, invented the first machine tool to produce standardized parts for muskets and laid the foundation for the interchangeability of parts. The United States long led the world in standardization, and many industrialists, engineers, and technicians believe that American standards are still the best in the world. There is in the United States an isolationist attitude toward international standardization—except on American terms—that influences the attitude toward the metric system: a mixture of aloofness, suspicion, apathy, and superiority.

In some instances, American standards are unquestionably the best in the world; the ABC screw thread standards represent the most complete and sophisticated system for fasteners and is recognized by the International Organization for Standardizaton. In other cases, American standards are the only standards. There are no metric standards for oil-field equipment; all such equipment in the world is made to American inch-pound standards. There are no international standards for lock-nuts; U.S. standards prevail everywhere. Automobiles produced in metric countries use tires made to inch-pound standards. On the other hand, American cars use spark plugs produced to metric standards. In the early days of the automobile industry, the American ceramics industry could not produce acceptable spark plugs, so they were imported from France and the metric standards to which they were made still prevail.

In the aviation industry, American standards are virtually universal around the world because of the leadership of the United States in airplane development and production. Likewise, in all nations of the world nautical miles are used for air navigation and air speeds, are given in knots, although neither of these are metric units. Some metric countries give flying heights in meters but French military and commercial planes have altimeters calibrated in feet because they are easier to read than those graduated in meters, and thus reduce the probability of pilot error.

There is a basic conflict between European and American standards that is independent of a measuring system. In Europe, and many metric countries elsewhere that have adopted the European system, most series of things have been sized for standardization by Preferred Numbers derived from geometric progression. These numbers were developed in the early stages of industrialization by a man named Renard and are often referred to as R numbers. In the United States, sizes for most things that are standardized in series were derived from fractions or by other means. Regardless of the system of measurement used, the systems of standardization are basically incompatible; to arrive at universal standards there will have to be compromise.

In recent years, there has been a coalition of effort outside the United States to develop metric standards that, in some areas, may be better than American standards. In many instances, the new metric standards make for economy by providing for less variety. Through the European Committee for the Co-ordination of Standards all of the countries of western Europe, Scandinavia, and some Communist bloc countries are working to create uniform and universal standards. Although the United States is a member of the International Organization for Standardization, its participation has been, in the words of a European member, "of an order significant to United States industry only in some fields."

Outside of Europe, all of the countries that are progressing industrially are increasingly using co-ordinated metric standards wherever they apply. This trend embraces highly industrialized Japan, India, the Latin American states, and the emerging nations of Africa. They still use American standards for automobile tires, airplanes, oil-field equipment, and many other things—and the majority of products throughout the world are still held together with inch thread fasteners. But in the "long swing of time," as Winston Churchill phrased it, the use of American standards will decrease.

All standard setters, American and foreign, are obsessed with whole numbers or nicely rounded-off numbers in establishing dimensions, and this makes compromise difficult. The bolt holes in the base of an American-produced motor may be 2 inches apart or, in metric terms, 5.08cm. Europeans do not want holes 5.08cm apart—they want a nice whole number: 5cm. Americans want the standard for a certain size of lumber to be 2″ × 4″, which would be 50.8mm × 101.6mm. Metric standard makers do not like these odd figures. Their standard for the same piece of lumber is 50mm × 100mm. In this case the standard is merely nominal; the actual dimensions of the product are smaller so that either standard would apply. In most cases this is not true. Americans might not object to calling a half-inch metal shaft 12.7mm, but they do not want to change to the ISO standard of 12.5mm. This negates interchangeability—a 12.7mm shaft will not fit a 12.5mm hole.

Modules have become very significant in modern technology. Under American standards, modules are based on measurements that can be simply expressed in inch-foot dimensions; foreign modules are dimensioned so as to be easily expressed in simple metric units. Obviously, modules made to American standards do not co-ordinate with those made to metric standards; 3 one-meter containers will not fit in a truck body that is 9 feet wide, nor do 3 one-yard containers efficiently use the space in a truck 3 meters wide. The International Organization for Standardization seems to be more willing than American standard setters to compromise. Four of the six sizes for international shipping containers that they have endorsed are based on inch-foot measurements.

American reluctance to compromise on standards is a salient point in the metric controversy. It took years of negotiation for the United States to reach agreement with its allies in NATO on a standard rifle bullet that could be used in the weapons of all nations. Finally the United States agreed to a metric standard of 7.62mm—which was not much of a compromise since the metric bullet is exactly equivalent to the U.S. .30 caliber bullet.

A prime subject of dispute in the metric controversy has been, and still is, the cost of conversion. There has been endless argument on this, all of it utterly futile because nobody has the slightest idea how much it will cost. Nor can costs be determined until the extent of conversion is decided upon and a time span established. There is a ratio of cost to time that works two ways. The most expensive type of conversion would be a crash program to convert everything overnight. But it would also be uneconomical to drag the conversion out over an unduly extended period, prolonging such transitional phases as dual dimensioning of engineering drawings, double inventories, storage and training problems, and the need for producing materials to standards of both systems. The most important contribution of the Department of Commerce survey will be to clarify costs under alternative assumptions as to time and extent.

The cost of conversion has been estimated by antimetrics at various figures ranging up to $100 billion. According to General Motors, conversion to the metric system would be so costly that it is unthinkable. A Ford Motor Company spokesman told a group of standards officials that the cost could conceivably be one-sixth to one-fifth of his company's capital worth. General Electric has estimated a more conservative $200 million for its changeover, which would represent about 4 percent of sales in conversion were accomplished in a single year. Other estimates are as high as 50 percent of annual sales. The chief designer for a machine tool builder claims that the cost of converting engineering drawings from inch to metric measurements would be as much as one-third the cost of making the original drawings. A statistician has figured out that there are some 2 million hand micrometers in the United States, each worth about $15. The cost of replacing this small item would be $30 million.

The most extreme cost estimates have all come from companies or industries in which costs would be highest and which are most opposed to conversion because they see little immediate gain. It is not clear which came first—opposition to the metric system or pessimism as to costs. A cynical observer might wonder whether some of this anguish on the part of industry may be aimed at laying a foundation to demand that government absorb part or all of the costs of conversion by tax abatement or some other means.

In India and Japan it has been found that cost estimates made before the fact have been virtually meaningless because they were many times higher than actual expenses. In England, Col. J. S. Vickers, Chief Engineer of the British Standards Institute, reported that, as of the end of 1969, "It is clear, as more and more firms are discovering, that the misgivings they had a couple of years ago are unfounded and the difficulties associated with this change are by no means as formidable as had been expected. . . . Two of our very large industrial firms who have, for good commercial reasons, adopted the metric system in advance of the national programmes are reporting 15 percent savings in design time as a result of the use of SI."

In the United States, those companies that have introduced the metric system to some extent, and have experience records rather than estimates, have not found costs to be extreme in relationship to the advantages. These include such industrial giants as Ford, Honeywell, and Deere.

The pharmaceutical industry, which has almost completely

converted to the metric system, is the only industry that has exact records on costs. Admittedly, this industry is one in which conversion costs are relatively low, but pharmaceutical companies found that actual expenses were much lower than estimates and that they were more than compensated for the savings even during the conversion period. Typical of the experience in this industry was that of Eli Lilly and Company, which spent some $13,000 for equipment and training and gained *annual* savings in excess of this amount in the cost of computation of formulations and inventory control. No dollar value can be assigned to the reduction in the possibilities of error.

The impact of increased metric usage will vary greatly in different industries. As a basis for cost studies, the Metric Study Group of the Bureau of Standards has classified all industry into five categories in which they label the cost of conversion as negligible, slight, moderate, substantial, or severe.

The negligible group includes such industries as agriculture, forestry, fishing, apparel, finance and insurance, mining, rubber and plastics, tobacco. In some of these, measured sizes of objects are not important; others would merely need to make a paper conversion of bulk commodities from pounds to kilograms, gallons to liters, etc.

The industries in which the impact would be slight include chemicals, furniture, lumber and wood products, paper, petroleum refining, printing and publishing, glass, textiles, etc. In these industries conversion would involve such changes as relabeling products, replacing simple measuring devices such as rulers and thermometers, changing dials on scales and gauges, etc.

All of the primary metal industries are in the moderate classification. Here conversion would require the replacement of complex measuring devices and the maintenance of dual inventories.

The substantial category includes industries that produce machinery, motors, or transportation equipment, including automobiles. Conversion in these industries would involve extensive costs in redesigning products and changing metal-forming machinery and stock sizes. The complex problem of screw fasteners also applies here.

In the severe classification conversion is described as "of such impact as to make change disastrous or inadvisable." This category includes the production of oil-field equipment and air and railroad transportation. Conversion is impractical here either because nonmetric practices are virtually world-wide or because new items of equipment must interface with old equipment that has a very long life.

Most of the estimates of unbearable costs come from companies in the moderate or substantial categories—but these industries produce only 11 percent of the gross national product. Eighty-nine percent of things produced in the United States come from industries in which the impact of conversion would be negligible or slight.

The high cost estimates seem to be based on the assumption that conversion will be total and will involve the immediate replacement of very expensive machinery and measuring devices. Neither of these assumptions is valid. Conversion will take place over an extended period during which much machinery can be replaced as it wears out or becomes obsolete. In many, perhaps most, instances, conversion can be accomplished by adjustment of machinery or replacement of minor parts, rather than replacing the whole machine.

Speaking at a meeting of the Standards Engineers Society, an economist from the Stanford Research Institute described how some of the cost estimates were arrived at. He said, "I think that many of the published cost estimates for conversion from inch to metric are much too high. They are not padded or distorted, but neither are they adjusted to conversion as it will actually happen. For example, you make a study in your company to see what it will cost to convert. Each division manager gathers thorough reports on the cost to adjust or replace each item in his plant that measures, weighs, has a gauge or dial, or is a document about these. The aggregate may be fairly accurate for *total immediate conversion*. But that is not the way conversion will happen. If each of these same division managers were told that conversion would begin today and would continue, say, 7 years—and that he had to convert at one-tenth of what he had estimated complete instantaneous conversion would cost—he not only could do it, but could perhaps do better."

This economist also questioned the estimates on the cost of redimensioning engineering drawings, which has been placed as high as one-third the cost of making the original drawings. Drawings that apply to current production represent a very small percentage of the total of such documents in any company's files, and these are the only ones that might need to be redimensioned to use the metric system. Most of the older drawings are seldom used and these would not need to be redimensioned for the dual-input machine tools that will be available during the transition period. Also, modern technology calls for an increasing use of numerically controlled automated equipment, and computers can be programmed from either inch or metric drawings.

The Stanford Research Institute made a study of the cost of conversion in 1962 and came up with an overall figure of $11 billion. This was based on the contention that much replacement could be done when machines became obsolete and that most machine tool controls could be very simply and inexpensively converted without replacing the machine. There is already on the market a machine tool dual-reading device in which a separate dial reading in metric units is geared to the original inch dial so that a complete revolution of both dials shows an even number of units in either system. This Stanford study estimated that the total cost of converting the 3½ million machine tools in the United States would be under $800 million.

Another factor that the high estimates do not take into consideration is that complex machines can be converted by replacing relatively inexpensive tools within the machine rather than by replacing the machine itself. The American

National Standards Institute analyzed what would be involved in converting a very expensive automated machine for making nuts and bolts by the cold forming process. In this machine the product is actually formed by what the Institute called "perishable tools"; the parts of the machine that handle the metal wear out after a short use and have to be replaced periodically. These perishable tools are available in metric to interface with the inch dimensions of the machine and cost no more than inch tools. "In processes of this type," said the report, "additional costs for metric parts should be minimal as far as the manufacturing processes are concerned, since a single machine can be used to produce parts of different configurations with an interchange of short-life tools."

American industry attained its superior position through the liberal application of what has been called "Yankee ingenuity," the use of imagination and innovation to create new things and new ways of doing things. This attitude is not apparent in the negative position of many industries on conversion; little creative thought has been given to ways in which conversion costs can be minimized. When people are actually faced with the problem imagination and ingenuity will surely be applied and various means will be developed to cut costs and improve efficiency and economy. In England, Col. Vickers reported that "A great many of the expected difficulties are in the event amenable to simple solutions."

One pharmaceutical company in the United States estimated that it would cost $125,000 to rewrite its formulas in metric terms. When the time came to actually spend the money, they gave it some more thought and realized that formulas were routinely reviewed and revised every 2 years and that they could be converted when they were normally recast with a negligible amount of added man-hours. Instead of spending more money, they actually saved money because the cost of recasting formulas is much less with simplified metric calculations.

With the space age, the words "software" and "hardware" have come into use to describe different aspects of industrial operations. Hardware covers physical, material things; software covers all kinds of paper work—statistical computations, inventory control, data processing, computer programming, and much more. The increase in this type of industrial activity under modern technology has been termed the "information explosion." Every year, the ratio of white collar workers to blue collar workers increases. The advantages of the metric system for software are so obvious that nobody seriously argues against it in this area and here the costs of conversion are negligible, limited largely to training expenses. One pro-metric analyst believes that "A change to metric could be a disguised blessing that would facilitate a step change in the art of data creation, use, storage, and retrieval. It was this philosophy of innovation which historically put the United States ahead of other countries, and I submit that this is a more important heritage than the inch."

None of the cost estimates takes into consideration compensating savings. In hardware, these may not be immediately apparent; the measuring system used will not affect the cost of production. In software, there will be a tremendous saving in man-hours through simplified computations and easier communications. Much costly skilled professional time is now wasted in communications between people in research and development who use the metric system and those in production who use the inch-pound. For the aerospace industry, the total is several hundred thousand man-hours per year. The U.S. Weather Bureau estimates that at least 1,000 man-hours a month are wasted in its operations by the need for routine conversions between the two systems.

There may well be a very considerable saving in hardware through the revision of standards that is necessary to metrication, both through the co-ordination of sizes under the new system and through a decrease in variety. Unified standards on hardware for the Department of Defense would effect great economy. Since World War I, when the United States adopted the French 75mm field gun, Army artillery and its ammunition have been produced to metric dimensions. Navy guns and ammunition are produced to inch dimensions. Rifles, machine guns, and side arms are dimensioned by caliber and shotguns by gauge; four different measuring systems are used in the production of these weapons. Obviously there would be a saving if all weapons were dimensioned by the same system.

In some industries where measurements involve only paper work, savings will be substantial. Agriculture is a case in point. Crop prices and statistics are based on bushels, grain storage is based on cubic feet, shipping costs are based on weight in tons. Since there is no logical relation between these three units in the Customary System, constant conversion is necessary, involving an enormous waste of man-hours. Under the metric system, the only units involved would be the kilogram and the cubic meter. Because of the simple relationship of these basic units the only conversion involved would be placing a decimal point.

Another factor that relates to conversion costs is the added profit and additional employment that would result in some businesses and industries. The company that buys a new metric tool may consider the purchase as an undesirable expense; to the company that makes and sells the tool the transaction represents a very desirable increase in volume and profits. The makers of all kinds of measuring instruments will benefit from conversion. The printing, publishing, and paper industries may expect a considerable increase in business from the production of new text books, manuals, catalogs, etc. Conversion will not constrict employment in any industry; an element in the complaint about costs is the additional man-hours of labor involved in adapting machinery and training personnel. In a few industries employment will substantially increase during the conversion period.

A final point in connection with costs, which is seldom mentioned, is that conversion is a one-time expense; the savings from conversion will continue year after year. To cite a purely hypothetical example, if it cost $1 billion a year over a 10-year period to convert and savings of one-half that amount were realized the conversion would be paid for in

20 years and thereafter the savings would be clear profit. Since it is certain that the software aspect of industrial production will continue to become relatively more important and that metrication will effect tremendous savings in this area, savings from conversion can be expected to increase in future years.

The second most important aspect of the Department of Commerce study may be the information that it will make available on the effect of the use of the inch-pound system in foreign trade. As in all other aspects of the metric controversy, there has been a wide variety of opinion on this, none of it based on reliable information. One economist claims that the United States is losing $10 billion a year in exports because of nonmetric usage. An estimate of $25 billion annual loss was expressed on the Senate floor.

Metric opponents claim that the principal cause of any loss in foreign business is high labor costs, not a system of measurements. They also point out that exports represent only about 4 percent of the gross national product and that most exports are bulk commodities that are not materially affected by measurements. Antimetrics also contend that American manufacturers would have more to lose than to gain if we switched because they would be faced with competition from manufacturers abroad who have lower labor costs. Adoption of the metric system would enable foreign industry to increase its competition in United States markets because its products could be serviced with locally made parts.

In the early stages of its study the Department of Commerce compiled preliminary comparative figures on total imports of metric and nonmetric countries for the period from 1960 to 1966 and the percentage that came from the United States. Since measurements are not important in connection with many commodities exported by the United States, the study established a separate category of comparison for machinery and transportation equipment, for which measurements are a factor. This separation affords a better basis for assessing the effects of nonmetric usage by the United States on foreign trade because the measurement system used does not appreciably affect bulk products like fuels and grains, whereas machinery is less desirable if it is not manufactured to the units and standards of the country in which it is used because it is not locally repairable.

A brief analysis of the preliminary figures shows the following trend:

U.S. percentage of total imports of major world countries

1960—20.5  percent
1966—19.0  percent

U.S. share of machinery imports of major world countries

1960—35.5  percent
1966—31.1  percent

U.S. share of total imports of nonmetric countries

1960—27.4  percent
1966—30.4  percent

U.S. share of machinery imports of nonmetric countries

1960—54.2  percent
1966—58.2  percent

U.S. share of total imports of metric countries

1960—17.5  percent
1966—14.3  percent

U.S. share of machinery imports of metric countries

1960—27.6 percent
1966—20.6 percent

In summary, the United States share of total imports of metric countries *declined* about 18 percent from 1960 to 1966; over the same period the United States share of total imports to nonmetric countries *increased* about 11 percent. In terms of machinery, the United States share of imports to metric countries *declined* about 25 percent while the share of imports to nonmetric countries *increased* about 8 percent. It must be remembered that, as of the mid-1970's when conversion will be completed in most Commonwealth countries, there will be no nonmetric countries to export to, with the possible exception of Canada, which will probably follow the lead of the United States rather than England.

A far more comprehensive study will be necessary to shed any real light on the effect of nonmetric usage on foreign trade but these preliminary figures raise some questions that those who claim that the measurement system used is of no consequence in foreign trade may find hard to answer. Why have exports of things on which measurements are meaningful increased to nonmetric countries and decreased to metric countries? Why has the decline in the export of such products to metric countries been almost 2½ times as great as the decline in total exports? Since exports to metric countries have declined while those to nonmetric countries have increased does not it seem reasonable that metric countries prefer to do business with other metric countries, including the Communist countries?

Competition in foreign trade between the United States and Communist countries is important in areas other than economics; with Communist trade may go Communist political philosophy. In this connection the relationship of the United States with its Latin American neighbors is of particular concern. The Director General of the Pan American Union said, "The United States loses business in Latin America because of persistence in using 'customary' weights and measures in exports which are not understood and do not fit in with the industrial economics of Latin Americans. In effect, we are trying to sell left-handed tools to people who are right-handed."

During the period studied by the Department of Commerce, total imports of the principal Latin American countries increased 15 percent. The United States share of total trade increased 6 percent, and Latin American imports of machinery from the United States increased only 2 percent. During a 5-year period—from 1963 to 1967—Latin American imports from Communist countries increased 20 percent, and most Communist exports are manufactured goods in which measurements are meaningful; Russian exports of bulk commodities to the western hemisphere are negligible. Russia *does* send Latin American countries translations of text books in mathematics and science; American books with inch-pound units are of little use to metric neighbors.

If the United States had been as successful in exporting to metric countries as it was in exporting to nonmetric countries, total exports for 1966 would have been $7 billion higher. Even the most ardent metric advocates do not claim that this increase would have been realized had the United States been using the metric system, but some part of the decline in business with metric countries is surely attributable to the difference in measuring systems.

The argument of the antimetrics that foreign trade is not important because it represents only 4 percent of the gross national product has little validity. Four percent of the level of production that is estimated during the 1970's is more than $40 billion a year, which is not a negligible amount. But regardless of whether the percentage is 4 or 40, maintaining it or, hopefully, increasing it is vital to correcting the balance of payments deficit. And with no nonmetric countries left to export to after the mid-1970's it is very unlikely that foreign trade could be maintained at even its present level if the United States clings to the isolationism of the inch-pound.

The effect of metrication on opening American markets to foreign metric imports is an unknown factor; no study has been made in this area. Metric countries do not seem to be hindered to any great extent in selling their products in the nonmetric United States. A comparison of imports from the United Kingdom and West Germany in recent years shows that metric Germany was more successful than nonmetric England in exporting to the United States; Japanese manufacturers also find a ready market for metric-dimensioned products in the United States. Some metric products might become more competitive with American-made products if they could be serviced and repaired with locally produced parts. This would hurt some American manufacturers; on the other hand, the increased competition might benefit the consumer.

The position of the metric system in the schools has changed significantly during the past decade. In years past, most schools gave students a fleeting exposure to the metric system in the upper elementary grades and almost invariably only in connection with conversion to or from Customary units. Mathematics text books posed such problems as, "1 kilometer = ⅝ of a mile. 16 kilometers = how many miles?" or "Use your centimeter ruler and an inch ruler to find out how many centimeters there are in 2 inches." The children did not really learn the metric system; they merely learned how to convert a few metric units to the inch system. That is why, in 1965, 93 percent of adult grade school graduates told Gallup pollsters that they did not know what the metric system was.

It is very unlikely that any considerable percentage of today's grade school pupils would give such an answer. The metric system is being introduced earlier in the curriculum and most new text books do not stress conversion; some even direct the teachers to avoid conversion completely and consider the metric system as a separate entity. In its preliminary investigations, the Metric Study Group of the Bureau of Standards reviewed elementary mathematics text books from 15 publishers. They found that 80 percent of all the newer texts introduce the metric system by the sixth grade and handle it in a reasonably satisfactory manner. Most of these books were written in the mid-1960's. Since schools replace text books every five years on the average, youngsters of the 1970's will get at least a moderately satisfactory introduction to the metric system.

Practices vary in different school systems. Some schools are introducing the metric system parallel with the Customary System in the first or second grade but teaching it independently of the conventional system, using 30cm rulers and cubic centimeter blocks to teach linear measure. One series of second grade work books has 6″ and 15cm rulers printed on the first page. The children cut these out and measure various things pictured in the book in both inches and centimeters, but do not convert from one to the other. By the time they finish second grade they know that there are two measuring systems.

The Commission on Science Education of the American Association for the Advancement of Science has prepared a science program for kindergarten through sixth grade which uses the metric system exclusively. This program was exposed to about a million students on an experimental basis in 1968 and became commercially available during the following year. Any child who learns science from this material during the first 7 years of his school life will be well indoctrinated in the metric system.

Another factor in modern education that is preparing young Americans for metrication is the much vaunted "new math," in which base 10 numeration is given more prominence. Under this system of teaching, students become more at home in the decimal system and spend less time on the drudgery of fraction arithmetic. This change has caused many educators to doubt the estimates of the more ardent metric advocates that much time would be saved in teaching mathematics if the metric system were adopted. They point out that fractions will still have to be taught, probably to the same extent as they occupy in the new math. There will be some saving of time when children do not have to learn the many units of the Customary System and memorize their arbitrary relationships. Since metric units are used exclusively in science classes there will be a considerable saving of time when science teachers do not have to teach the metric system so that their pupils can understand texts in physics, general science, biology, and chemistry.

The metric system is used in the United States to a greater extent than is generally realized. The Bureau of Standards reports, "Over the past 100 years, the metric system has seen slow, steadily increasing use in the United States, and, today, is of importance nearly equal to the Customary System." Most people are exposed to the metric system repeatedly without realizing it. They buy medicines and drugs in metric measurements; they tune their radios to frequencies expressed in meters; by act of Congress, S.I. units are the *only* legal units for electricity and illumination; the labels on over 40 percent of packaged food products show metrics as well as avoirdupois weight; home movie makers buy film in metric widths.

The increased sale of foreign cars has exposed millions of motorists to all-metric products, and those who would repair their own may purchase a large assortment of metric tools in Sears, among other places. New Americans are born under the metric system—most hospitals keep birth records of weight and length in metric units. In fact, every American has been unwittingly using metric products every day since 1876—in that year the United States mint began using metric weights for coinage.

American scientists have used the metric system for decades. It is used exclusively in oceanography and optometry. Most research and development engineers use it, as do doctors and dentists. Science text books for schools are written in the metric system. Industrially, it is being increasingly used in varying degree, depending on the industry and the policies of individual companies. The pharmaceutical industry uses it almost exclusively, as does the electric power industry. It is used together with Customary units for hardware in the electronics, plastics, chemical, and photographic industries. Ball and parallel bearings are made to metric specifications, as are spark plugs.

There are many inconsistencies in metric usage. The width of motion picture film is measured in millimeters; the length is measured in feet. In pharmaceuticals, all measurements are expressed in grams, kilograms, milliliters, etc.; but companies in this industry must report their stocks of alcohol to the Internal Revenue Service in gallons.

Some industrial companies have converted to the extent of expressing dimensions on engineering drawings in both the metric and inch systems, including such giants as IBM and Deere & Co.; there is a pronounced trend toward metric usage among manufacturers of agricultural equipment. International Harvester, a leader in this field, believes "that there are now clear signs that industry in this country will be using S.I. units in the foreseeable future. Accordingly, we have developed a standard practice for introducing English and S.I. units simultaneously on our design drawings (dual dimensioning) and we are commencing on a limited basis to put this practice into effect."

The Ford Motor Company uses metric measurements in production only in Germany, but it employs a combination of inch-pound and metric units in 11 other countries where metric is the national system. Many of the testing operations of its engineering staff at Dearborn are conducted in metric units, as are its basic research activities. In Ford's paint plant, development work is formulated in metric units and converted to inch-pound units for quantity production. The Philco Division uses metric units in many of its activities and they are employed in production in the vinyl plant.

Ford's policy has heartened metric advocates. Heretofore the automobile industry, where conversion costs will be high, has been strongly opposed to conversion. It was therefore something of a breakthrough when the Vice-President of Engineering for Ford wrote to a Senate Commerce committee:

> The benefits of a single measuring system in a world-wide, interdependent economy are so great that we believe that the conversion to the Metric System is inevitable. Although there may be short term costs and confusion during such a far reaching change, the long term gains appear to be overwhelming for any country that expects to be an active participant in world commerce and trade. The basically simple structure of the Metric System also carries with it many substantial benefits, even for an isolated user. The magnitude of the conversion task in the automobile industry is such that any attempt at conversion on a crash basis would be chaotic, both physically and financially. On the other hand, a well-planned conversion can minimize both the cost and confusion, and permit the benefits of the system to be realized at the earliest possible date.

The Army has been shifting toward the metric system for several years and in 1966 announced an objective, "to establish a common unit of measurement in connection with the operation of all United States Army weapons, to facilitate standardization within NATO, to permit better and more extensive use of allied and captured enemy material, and to simplify firing procedures for indirect firing weapons." After January 1 of that year, "All United States Army and related equipment . . . will be designed to employ the meter as the unit of linear measure."

The Department of Defense has established a metric study group to support the Department of Commerce study. Apparently, Defense believes metric conversion to be inevitable for they are basing their study on the following assumptions:

> July 1, 1972—Adoption of the metric system by Congress. Use will be optional. Initiate training and data conversion.

July 1, 1977—Initiate procurement in the metric system. General use increasing but not mandatory. Training and conversion of technical data (manuals, specifications, and standards) completed.

July 1, 1982—Metric units mandatory in all DOD procurement. Replacement items still available in inch system.

Until very recently, metric conversion received little support from most sections of American industry. Today, there are signs of interest in the subject, but little enthusiasm. In a study reported in the organ of the American Society for Metals, industry's position was summarized thus: "A relatively few key companies in manufacturing have taken some interim steps toward the metric system. In most instances, they have operations in metric countries; and their action is largely confined to dual dimensioning. It should be noted that some members of this group are reluctant to report on their activities at this time."

There was still much active opposition to metric conversion within industry in the 1960's. When 119 engineers and production and inspection executives of 36 divisions of General Motors were asked, "Do you believe the advantages to be sufficient to warrant U.S. industry support of the metric system?" 107 replied in the negative, only 12 in the affirmative.

In 1965, the American Society of Mechanical Engineers stated:

The American Society of Mechanical Engineers, in the interest of national economy and industrial efficiency, advocates the continued use of the existing American, British, and Canadian sizes, modules, designs, and ratings. Further, the Society is of the opinion that legislative action directed to an alternate system of dimension standards, such as the metric, will be at this time confusing and disturbing to the productive capacity of the United States and is not, therefore, in the best of public interest.

As recently as 1967, the National Machine Tool Builders Association told a Senate committee that it

> . . . finds an overwhelming opinion among its members to continue the use of the "decimal-inch" system of measurement in the United States. In the opinion of United States Machine Tool Builders, there is no pressing need for, nor advantage in, a conversion to the metric system. To convert today would involve disruption of the overall production capacity of the United States and monumental confusion and unbearable costs to the United States metal working industry.

The isolationist attitude of some industrialists was typified by an executive of a fastener company, who said, "American business will never voluntarily switch to the metric system. As long as we're as dominant as we are, we can make the trend instead of going with it."

On the other side of the coin, some branches of engineering seem to be increasingly favorable toward conversion. The American Institute of Mining, Metallurgical and Petroleum Engineers "supports adoption of the metric (S.I.) system of measurements on a national basis." The American Society of Civil Engineers "will further, by all legitimate means, the adoption of metric standards in the office of weights and measures at Washington."

In a recent "Opinion Poll" taken by the magazine *Industrial Engineering*, almost 94 percent of the 3,100 scientists and engineers who responded favored the adoption of the metric system in the United States. An additional 3 percent favored partial adoption. Only 3 percent opposed. Approximately three-quarters of those who favored conversion felt that it should be mandatory in all industries; the others believed that it should be voluntary in each industry. In another survey made by *Design News,* which is read by design engineers, the responses were 80 percent for conversion and 20 percent against.

NASA endorsed the Department of Commerce metric study, "with the hope that it will lead to the institution of the metric system itself. The metric system is now the basic language of scientific measurement. . . . Standardization to the metric system would save the time and effort involved in translation measurements and in educating students in both systems. . . . The fast-growing use of computers has made fractions even more obsolete."

At a House committee hearing in 1969, the chairman observed that there had been vigorous resistance by industry to any thought of increased metric usage and asked Dr. A. V. Astin, Director of the National Bureau of Standards, whether there had been any recent change in attitude. Dr. Astin replied, "Yes, sir. One of the things that has impressed us most during this study phase has been the increased acceptance by industrial associations of the possible need for change toward the metric system. Many think it inevitable, and are interested in helping us to bring it about."

A survey of 39 industrial and engineering associations and societies made for this book does not entirely support Dr. Astin's optimism. The organizations queried were all groups that are concerned with standards for their industries or professions. Several of them expressed themselves as interested in the study that Commerce is making, and willing to cooperate in this work; but only 3 of the 39 favored conversion. Two of these have previously been quoted. The third, a scientific society, believed that most of its members favored conversion, but asked not to be quoted as formally endorsing the move.

An equal number of respondents were of the opinion that most of their members would not approve adopting the metric system: "I can frankly say that there is a great deal of reluctance to make the switch." "It is my personal opinion that even a partial adoption of the metric system in our industry will not be favored for at least a decade." "There does not seem to be any strong feeling as yet toward conversion to metrication."

The most significant result of this survey of industrial opinion on metric conversion is that industry does not seem to have an opinion—or, more exactly, industrial associations that might be expected to provide guidance do not want to express an opinion. Of the 39 queried, 31 either had no comment or no opinion. Typical responses were: "Our organization has not taken any position at this time in regard to conversion to the metric system." "At this moment we do not have an industry position." "Since the matter is presently under study, no position has been taken by this industry on conversion to the metric system. We do not wish to be quoted on any aspect of position other than that the matter is being studied by an Industry group." Several respondents mentioned that their organizations had appointed committees, or expected to do so, to co-operate in the Commerce study, and a few pointed out that since the metric matter was being studied it would be illogical to take a position until the study is completed.

From this survey and other sources two minor trends toward the metric system and metric standards seem to be evident. A number of associations have started to use metric units, together with inch-pound units, in their journals, standards, bulletins, and other technical publications. The American Society of Agricultural Engineers "considers it desirable and necessary for the profession to give greater recognition to metric units and thereby make its documents more understandable and useful to readers in both English and metric areas." Several other organizations expressed themselves in a similar vein.

The American Society for Testing and Materials, a nonprofit society devoted to the standardization of specifications and the methods of testing is in the process of introducing S.I. units alongside U.S. Customary units throughout its 25,000-page, 32-volume annual *Book of ASTM Standards*. The Society "believes it desirable and necessary that industry be prepared for wider use of the metric system," although "it does not now advocate or recommend any change in presently established dimensions or tolerances." The ASTM has not officially endorsed metric conversion but their metric program "stems from a belief in the inevitability of the S.I. system in the United States. Increasingly it seems to be not a question of 'whether' but of 'when.' Since it seems all but certain that metric units of measurements will one day be the common system in the United States, the Society believes it should do whatever it can to ease the eventual transition."

The other trend that has become apparent in the past year or two is a softening of the isolationist attitude toward international standards. There is a growing realization that the executive who said, "we can make the trend instead of going with it" is out of step with the times. American industry is not willing to scrap its own standards in favor of those of metric countries, but there is a growing realization that negotiation and compromise must replace the previous attitude of "this is it; take it or leave it." Through the American National Standards Institute, a nonprofit federation devoted to the development of voluntary standards, there are American members on 87 technical committees of the International Organization for Standardization. The Institute organized an International Standards Committee in 1969.

The move toward the metric system in industry and government is slowly gathering momentum. Many whose minds were completely closed to any consideration of change are now thinking about it—albeit, in many instances, reluctantly. In industrial associations and individual companies, personnel have been assigned to study how a change might be effected and what its impact would be. Increasingly in government, science, education, engineering, and from other informed sources the word "inevitable" is heard. Among thinking men there is almost unanimity of opinion that adoption of the metric system by the United States is inevitable.

# 8

# WHEN, HOW,
# AND HOW MUCH?

The United States is dedicated to a position of world leadership. It cannot maintain this position and stand alone clinging to a measuring system built upon the length of barley-corns and the girdles of Saxon kings. In the space age, the inch-pound system is as archaic as Roman numerals or cunei-form writing. It must go, and it will go. The problems facing the nation today are how the change will be made, when it will be made, and how much of a change is necessary or advantageous.

Because the United States in the past has taken an ostrich attitude toward the metric system—rather hoping that if we ignored it, it would go away—there is little concrete data on which to base answers to these questions. Hopefully, the Department of Commerce study will at least partially rectify this. But it is becoming increasingly obvious that if we do not act now our isolated position will force us to act later when all of the problems and costs will be magnified and when we may be compelled to adopt a program of crash conversion.

The reasons for changing have been covered in previous chapters of this book. To summarize briefly, the metric system has certain inherent advantages. Principally, it is easier to learn because of its decimal basis and its smaller number of logically related units. In the metric system, calculations of measurements are simpler, shorter, and less prone to error. The learning advantage applies equally to the school child who will no longer have to memorize the many unrelated units of the Customary System and devote endless hours to drills in fractions, and to the engineering student in college whose calculations will be simplified and for whom the definite, coherent S.I.-derived units are much easier to learn and apply. For measurement where calculation is involved, the advantages of the metric system apply equally to the man who is building a chicken coop or the man who is building a space capsule; to the woman who buys a box of detergent or the multibillion-dollar procurement activities of the Department of Defense.

The advantage of the metric system in education may be more far reaching than is readily apparent. In years past, it was considered important for a person to be literate; to be able to read and write. Today, it is becoming increasingly important for a person to be "numerate," to deal facilely with numbers, quantities, and calculations. This applies not only to scientists, technologists, and engineers; more and more aspects of management and government involve the kind of quantitive judgment that only the numerate possess. On the whole, Americans are not numerate. On television quiz shows on which the participants are presumably above the average intellectually, and which sometimes include brilliant high school and college students, the questions that are most frequently unanswered are those involving arithmetic.

Dr. M. F. Lighthill, Physical Secretary of the British Royal Society, has theorized that the reason why English-speaking people are not as numerate as they might be is that children become bored with arithmetic in the early grades of school. "The loss of able children to the world of numeracy as a result of sheer arithmetical boredom is the worst possible consequence of a proliferation of systems. Most harmful of all is the influence of this too-prolonged immersion in complicated arithmetical processes upon the *choices* pupils make between mathematical and other subjects at fourteen, fifteen and sixteen." America is short of engineers, technicians, and people equipped for positions in which quantitive appreciation is necessary because so many kids start to hate arithmetic at about the fourth grade. There is no evidence of such a shortage in Russia. The "new math" may avoid some of this boredom, but more progress in making arithmetic interesting is needed to equip the rising generation to meet the numeracy demands of modern society. The change in the teaching of arithmetic made possible by adopting the metric system would be a long step in this direction.

Another significant reason for changing to the metric system is to facilitate communications on two fronts. Maintaining a position of world leadership requires communication between the United States and the rest of the world. In terms of measurements, and all technology, engineering, and commerce in which they are used, communications is now possible only between scientists, who all use the metric system. National security is involved in the problems of communication with our allies. It is desirable in military strategy that armaments produced by allied countries be made interchangeable so that replacement parts and ammunition may be produced in different areas of the world.

On another front, communications between scientists and engineers is becoming ever more important. Nowhere is this more evident than in the space program. All progress in this area starts with the scientist and ends with the engineer who builds the hardware. These do not speak the same measurement language; nor are many research and development engineers in other industries, who are responsible for future progress, able to communicate freely with the production engineers who are responsible for making what R & D creates.

Converting from one system to the other is wasteful, confusing, and frought with the possibility of error. Recently, a young engineer substantially "increased" the estimated efficiency of a nuclear power plant by an error in converting kilograms to pounds; fortunately, he caught his mistake. In another instance, a discussion on the effect of sun spots on radio communication ground to a halt because one engineer used a metric formula and another an inch-pound one. A mathematician was called in to straighten things out; and *he* made a mistake in conversion.

In the software aspect of industry, which is constantly becoming more important under the new technology, the advantages of the metric system are so obvious that they do not need to be delineated. The smaller number of metric units, decimally related, make possible the saving of costly man-hours in such business functions as inventory control, the computation of formulae and engineering equations, the handling, storage, and interpretation of data, and much else.

The principal reason for a change goes beyond the advantages of the metric system. The United States cannot stay out of step with the rest of the world commercially and technologically, and our unique system of measurements puts us in this situation. In the past, the United States was in a favored position because of its superior technology, organization, and finances. But tomorrow's markets will be more competitive and, with the British Commonwealth countries metricized, specifications will become entirely metric and the rest of the world will insist on products produced to its system. Countries that are becoming increasingly industrialized will depend for advice and equipment on more advanced countries with which they have a common system.

If it is accepted that we must change—and all informed opinion agrees that change is inevitable—the question arises as to how the change should be brought about. Some die-hard inch-pound advocates still seek to avoid an outright change to the metric system. One expert in this camp has proposed a 7-point program that includes decimalization of existing inch units, expanded teaching of decimals in schools, revising the Customary System to eliminate archaic units, popularization of common metric terms such as kilowatt by replacing English terms with them, and adoption of scientific units in engineering practice.

Such proposals are comparable to going into cold water

a step at a time—it merely prolongs the agony. Decimalizing
the inch and eliminating pecks, rods, and furlongs will not
put the United States in step with the rest of the world. And it
is impossible to decimalize the inch system without eliminating
the foot, the yard, the rod, the furlong, and the mile—none
of which bears a decimal relation to the inch. While sugges-
tions for halfway measures are still heard, they become less
frequent as more serious and constructive study is given to the
problem.

It is becoming generally accepted that the only feasible
change is to the metric system or, more specifically, the S.I.
version of the metric system. Metric advocates were heartened
when a representative of the fastener industry, for which a
change presents great problems, admitted this. At a Senate
committee hearing, R. B. Belford, representing the Industrial
Fasteners Institute, said that his organization "believes in a
one-world system of measurement." When asked by Senator
Pell whether such a system might be along the lines of the
former English system, Mr. Belford replied, "I think that
any technical man in this country who has been exposed intimately would have to realize that if the whole world was
going to work toward one system of weights and measures
then it must be the metric system."

There are many views as to how the metric system should
be adopted. In the Senate hearing referred to above, Senator
Pell said, "In order for a country to go on the metric system,
it would probably have to be mandatory, because that is
the experience of history." While it is true that almost every
country that has metricized has done so by government edict,
with the significant exception of England, it seems inconceivable that Congress, in the near future, will rule that, as
of a certain date, all weights and measures in the country
must be metric. Such a law would be no more popular than
Prohibition and would present even more complex enforcement problems.

In hearings on the Pell bill, Dr. Astin of the Bureau of
Standards made the point that

It is important to understand that our choice is not simply between total mandatory conversion and total inaction. Numerous other alternatives are open for consideration including:

(a) Voluntary extension of metric usage, industry by industry—possibly with a system of financial incentives to those who convert.

(b) Regulated partial conversion, segment by segment, in identified areas over an extended period of time.

(c) Solutions other than adoption of the metric system to mitigate crucial problems.

The industry-by-industry method of conversion does not seem feasible because few industries are independent of other industries. An expert from the Department of Commerce made this point by saying, "Our modern technological economy is made up of a complex network of producing, distributing, and consuming units. In only a few instances would it be possible for a single business or firm to make a change to the metric system on its own initiative without a simultaneous change by other firms or businesses. Some industries may be represented by a simple flow chart from producer of raw materials, to manufacturer, to distributor, to consumer. Here at least the first three parties would have to agree on a change."

As an instance, assume that the agricultural implement industry, to which foreign markets are important, wants to metricize. Their products require materials and components from a score of other industries—metals, rubber, electrical parts, plastics, paint, and glass, to mention a few. The agricultural implement industry could not produce efficiently to metric specifications unless these other industries could supply materials and parts to metric dimensions. And they would need metric tools. It would not be economically feasible for the steel industry to produce metric-dimensioned rods for the agricultural implement industry and a very similar inch-dimensioned rod for the automobile industry, although this may be necessary during a transitional period.

One opinion on how the change to metric might transpire was expressed by Dr. A. G. McNish when he was chief of the Metrology Division of the National Bureau of Standards. The view is of particular interest because Dr. McNish now heads up the Metric Study Group at the Bureau. He said, "It is likely the solution to this problem will be found by establishing international specifications including allowable sizes some of which are inch-based and some metric-based for products already in extensive use. . . . It is the writer's personal opinion that the United States will change over to S.I. gradually, that our systems of Customary Units will slowly be phased out. Hardheaded American industrialists will not suffer themselves to be discommoded by a measurement system imposed on them by edict. Neither will these same hardheaded industrialists permit themselves to be denied the advantages of an improved measurement system, particularly if such denial forces them into an inferior position in contending for the world's markets. During this transition period which is now upon us there will be increasing use of S.I. units in science and engineering. Old professors will learn it and new students will be taught it. They will think in S.I. and design in S.I. although for some time their designs must be translated into the inch system for production by American industry." The paper from which this is quoted was delivered in 1965, before England and other Commonwealth countries had signified their intention of going metric; an event that may have much influence on the speed of conversion in the United States.

There is considerable opinion that the transition in the United States will parallel that in England, which has previously been described. But it must be realized that there is one great difference between the situations in the two countries. In England, the impetus to change came from industry, which requested government support. England's foreign trade in manufactured goods is so important that it was a question of either change or starve. This is not true in the United States. Because foreign trade is much less important to American industry it almost certainly will not take the initiative in changing to the metric system. A parallel might be drawn between the attitude of industrial leadership toward metrication and its attitude toward labor unions in the early 1930's. There was a general reluctance to accept the principle of unionism, just as there is toward accepting the metric system. It required a countrywide wave of strikes, coupled with strong support of labor by the federal government, to convince management that unionism was inevitable. Government influence was applied through executive orders and favorable, but not mandatory, legislation with the result that over a period of about 10 years most manufacturing industry became unionized.

If a change is to be accomplished in measuring systems, the impetus and leadership will have to come from government. Also, the change will be so complex that detailed, co-ordinated planning will be necessary. In view of industry's attitude toward conversion it is unlikely that this planning will be undertaken by any private industrial organization; nor is it conceivable that any private organization could be formed with a breadth of interest and membership representing all of the sectors that would be affected by metrication. It is logical that planning will be co-ordinated by government through an agency similar to England's Committee on Metrication. This agency may have some authority to compel compliance. In any event, government will ultimately be able to exert pressure through its own procurement procedures; issuing metric specifications requiring that potential contractors submit proposals in metric terms and that products purchased by the government meet metric testing standards and be packaged in metric units. Considering the extent of government purchasing, few important manufacturers would refuse to compete on these terms.

The Air Force made a move in this direction a few years ago by requesting bids from two contractors for the production of the Maverick missile in metric dimensions. The prices quoted were so much higher than production to inch dimensions that the idea was abandoned and the missile was produced by the inch system. However, it might be said that the conditions of bidding were "rigged" in favor of the inch. The proposals included the cost of converting machinery to the metric system to produce the missile and converting it back to the inch system after the contract was completed. Further, since this would take time, a cost of living increase clause was inserted so that prices would rise with the passage of time.

Another aspect of the changeover question on which there is a wide variety of opinion is the length of time the change may require. There is a popular belief that a decision to convert would involve the immediate launching of a crash program under which meters and kilograms would replace inches and pounds overnight. Such groundless fears were fostered by antimetrics who never mentioned any other alternative and played up the havoc that such a change would cause. Most informed opinion holds that conversion will probably be spread over a 10- or 20-year period, with 10 years having the preference. The Department of Defense is basing its study on a 10-year conversion assumption.

If the 10-year premise is accepted, there is some theorizing that significant conversion may be accomplished by 1985. This is based on the assumption that Congress will take 4 years to act on the report of the Metric Study Group—perhaps an optimistic view when it is considered that the legislators took 7 years to pass the metric study bill.

In 1963, Stanford Research Institute concluded its study on the cost of conversion with this ferecast: "It is anticipated that, by the year 2000, the United States will have changed from its Customary System of measurement to the metric system. The change, which has already begun, will accelerate in the 70's. Within 20 to 30 years, half of U.S. industry will be on the metric system; within 50 years, the present system will probably be obsolete." This prediction did not contemplate that England would break the inch-pound bloc. In view of all that has happened since 1963, the Stanford timetable is probably too slow.

However, unless some pressure is applied, conversion could drag out for decades. Consider the action of the National Research Council in making a minor change from Fahrenheit to Celsius temperature scales. In 1960, a few members of the Aerospace Materials Division of the Society of Automotive Engineers requested that temperatures in aerospace material specifications be expressed in Celsius instead of Fahrenheit because several government agencies, notably NASA, required that Celsius temperatures be used in technical documentation. After thinking about this for a few months it was decided to adopt a 3-step program. The first step was inaugurated a year later. This involved adding equivalent Celsius temperatures in parenthesis after Fahrenheit temperatures in specifications. The second step, reversing the position and putting Celsius temperatures first with Fahrenheit in parenthesis, was started 3 years later. The third step will be the elimination of Fahrenheit temperatures but "it will be many years before this phase can be incorporated. This must follow education and re-education of engineers, metallurgists, chemists, technicians, and even mechanics to think in terms of Celsius temperatures." Under this method, the third step in the change may not take place until a new generation of engineers, technicians, and mechanics that does not know the Fahrenheit scale comes on the scene.

Obviously, it should not take more than 10 years to educate even the most backward mechanic in the Celsius scale. He need merely consult a child's encyclopedia to learn the simple conversion equation: $F = 1.8C + 32$. Getting him to *think* Celsius is a different problem, and it is unlikely that he will ever learn to think Celsius so long as the Fahrenheit figures are published. This very slow progress, more than a decade for a simple change, indicates that constructive effort, propaganda, and perhaps some pressure will have to be applied to effect an overall change.

The metric study bill does not contain the words "conversion" or "adoption." Its purpose is to study the effect of "increasing the use of metric weights and measures in the United States."

This will undoubtedly lead to conversion, but the transition will probably involve several steps. The Metric Study Group has delineated three degrees of increased usage, which they have labeled *accommodation, adaptation,* and *conversion.*

Accommodation is described as the response that an individual who is little concerned with measurements might make; it is comparable to that of a tourist traveling in a metric country. When metric units are introduced this will be the initial response of most people, who will continue to use household scales calibrated in pounds and recognize that the new kilogram is about 2.2 lbs. In businesses where exact measurements are not important, measuring equipment need not be changed and approximate conversion tables may be used to transfer from customary to metric units.

A word about conversion tables. Experience has shown that exact conversion tables retard the acceptance of the metric system because they make it seem very complicated. In a table that shows Customary units in round numbers and their metric equivalents the latter usually contain from 4 to 8 or 9 digits: 1 yd. = 0.9144m, 1 qt. = 0.946353 l, or 1 lb. = 0.453592 kg. Where precision is not involved, simpler approximate conversion tables are usually satisfactory: 1 yd. = 0.9m, 1 qt. = 0.95 l, 1 lb. = 0.45 kg.

Adaptation, the second degree of response, is required in cases where there is a considerable contact with units of measurements. It involves double marking of containers; sizes or quantities may not be changed but the containers are marked in round numbers of Customary units with the metric equivalent. In industry it involves dual dimensioning on drawings so that a part can be made with either metric or inch machines. Where translations are too much of a chore, measuring devices may be recalibrated in metric units or in both systems. The important aspect of adaptation is that the measurements of things do not change but they are described in metric language. In any program of change, the general adoption of metric language will be essential.

Adaptation is already in progress; many food containers are marked in both systems, and industry is making increased use of dual dimensioning. It may continue to be the principal response during a transition period, but it cannot be the ultimate solution. Adaptation is, in a sense, merely paying lip service to the metric system; it does not make American products compatible with those made elsewhere in the world. Also, in industry, it represents added expense without compensating advantages, since it obviously costs more to dimension a drawing in two systems than in one. In addition, closer tolerances are usually set on dual-dimensioned drawings to assure compatibility of parts when dimensions are translated from one system to the other, and this results in increased costs.

Conversion is the ultimate response to increased metric usage. Theoretically, it assumes that no other system exists. Goods are packaged and sold in round numbers of metric units. Things are designed in metric units. Standards are based on round numbers of metric units. Material is made in metric stock sizes. This is the only response that will create a universal system of weights and measures and that will make U.S. products compatible with those made elsewhere in the world.

In analyzing the impact of a change to the metric system, industry must base their calculations on some assumption of how the change will take place. The American National Standards Institute has prepared an orientation guide for companies in the mechanical products industries. The guide presents three alternative assumptions.

The first assumption is of a crash program for immediate conversion to metric units and ISO metric standards. The result of this assumption, says the guide, "is likely to be financial and physical chaos which no company could afford. This assumption is to be avoided."

The second course is to assume that new products would be designed to metric modules "before metric standard parts and materials are readily available. . . . This would result in a necessity to redesign as new metric standard parts and materials become available, resulting in non-interchangeability with the original metric design and a multiplicity of inventory during the transition period which would extend over many years. The interim steps in this assumption would be quite costly and accomplish little."

The third choice is to assume that new products and components that require special tooling would be specified in metric modules "only after new metric standard parts and materials are readily available at reasonable costs. This could be accomplished on an optimum schedule as present product designs become obsolete on a timetable compatible with marketplace requirements and normal tool obsolescence. Such a plan would result in minimal costs." The third assumption is obviously the only reasonable one and is undoubtedly that which will be most frequently used in a changeover.

But before metric parts and materials can be produced, metric standards for these parts and materials must be developed and this may well be the most complex and lengthy operation in conversion to the metric system. To repeat, standards and measuring systems are different things; a standard in either system can be expressed in units of the other measuring system. It would be a simple matter to translate the ABC fastener standards into metric language—but that would not make a 12.7mm bolt fit a 12.5mm hole. Interchangeability is based on uniform standards rather than on a measuring system; a half-inch bolt would fit a 12.7mm hole.

Bringing the United States in line with the rest of the world in terms of the interchange of manufactured products will require an agreement on internationally accepted standards. The chief engineer of the Ford Motor Company said, "If the determination is made that it is in the best interests of the United States to expand the use of S.I. units in this country, commercial standards organizations . . . must move toward the review of existing standards on an international basis. It cannot be assumed that all industries and standard-making bodies in this country would be willing to accept all existing metric standards as they are now written."

Another objective of the metric study bill is to determine

how and to what extent American standards may be retained and promoted for international use. While the contention that all American standards are the best in the world is not entirely warranted, it is true that the United States has in the past gone farther in this direction than any other country and many of its standards systems are unquestionably superior. In such cases, it would be unthinkable to scrap American standards as a prelude to adopting the metric system of measurement.

Developing international standards will require a long period of negotiation, with America trying to sell its standards for international adoption in metric language. This will result in a certain amount of give and take. In the past, the United States has been reluctant to give. This attitude is less pronounced today and there will undoubtedly be a greater willingness to compromise in the future.

Threaded fastener standards are a case in point. Screws and bolts are used by every mechanical industry in every country in the world. Until a single international set of standards is developed for fasteners, complete compatibility of mechanical products cannot be achieved. The United States has one system based on inch units, the Unified Thread System, called ABC because it was accepted by the United States, Britain, and Canada in an accord signed in 1948. In the past, several sets of metric fastener standards have been used in various countries. The International Organization for Standardization has clarified metric standards by adopting one set. The Organization also approves the ABC standards, but these two standards are not comparable. Future negotiation may well develop an entirely new set of fastener standards that will probably be very similar to the ABC system because this is unquestionably the most sophisticated. When this millennium arrives, any screw or bolt made anywhere in the world will fit the fastener holes in any product made anywhere in the world; the farmer in West Germany who needs a bolt to repair his American-made tractor can buy one made in Hamburg, he will not have to get one made in the U.S.A. These new standards will be expressed in metric terms—but that is really immaterial.

Considering the complexity of revising standards where international agreement is desirable, the estimate of 20 years for the achievement of significant conversion may be more realistic than the 10-year estimate that is more frequently quoted.

Once metric standards are established, the next important step in industrial conversion will be to change production of materials and standard parts to metric dimensions. Obviously, there would be no point in designing an engine that requires a 20mm piston pin unless the metal industries can deliver a rod from which a 20mm pin can be economically produced. The problems and costs of conversion of materials will vary greatly for different types of substances. In general, the conversion to metric dimensions of materials made in sheets—metals, plastics, paper, plywood, etc.—will be relatively simple. Thickness can be changed merely by adjusting rollers, width and length by recalibrating gauges and measuring devices. Materials and parts that are formed by casting, stamping, or machining operations will present greater and more costly problems because of necessary changes in dies and tooling.

Even in this area, the few manufacturers who now produce to the metric system have found the transition to be much easier than most predictions. One of the leading fastener manufacturers, the Standard Pressed Steel Company, produces in both systems here and abroad. Its plant in Coventry, England, switched 25 percent of its production to meet that country's early demand for metric screws without too much difficulty. Said Standard's technical vice-president, "Our own experience, in both our domestic and overseas plants, has proved to us that it is no more difficult to produce threaded fasteners to the metric system than to the inch system, once the learning process has been completed."

The problems of conversion in software are relatively minor compared to those of hardware. In the main, they involve training people to work and think in the metric system. India, Japan, and England—and the pharmaceutical industry in the United States—have found that this is not as difficult as had been anticipated.

In some industries, conversion would primarily involve software changes; and the products of these industries represent the greatest dollar value and the largest quantity of American production. These include all materials that are sold in bulk: agricultural products, construction materials (such as cement, sand, gravel, and plaster), chemicals, paint, fertilizers, coal, oil, gas, etc. The only physical change required to convert to the metric system at the wholesale level for such products would be a recalibration of measuring instruments. In some cases, the change at the retail level would be more costly, involving metric-dimensioned containers and changing many measuring devices; all gasoline pumps would have to be changed from gallons to liters, for instance.

For public utilities, other than transportation, conversion will be primarily a software problem in record keeping and billing. In the gas industry, meters will have to change from cubic feet and, if the S.I. system is strictly followed, electric meters should change from kilowatt-hours to joules. However, this can be a software conversion until the meters are normally replaced. Telephone service is expressed in dimensionless units and would not be affected.

A change to metric standards and language would have little or no effect on some products. These include things that are designated by numbered sizes that are not the actual dimensions, or products for which the standard dimensions are nominal and do not express the actual size. Wire sizes are given in numbers that bear no relation to any system of units; some women's dress sizes are expressed in numbers that do not relate to measurements; size twelve, fourteen, etc.; a ten-penny nail will probably continue to be a ten-penny nail when it is produced by the metric system. The actual dimensions of steel pipe differ from the nominal dimensions and could be equally expressed in round numbers in either centimeters or inches without changing the size of the pipe. The same is true for planed lumber; the actual size of scantlings would remain the same whether they are called 2x4's or 50x100's—only the length would change.

For many consumer goods, adaptation will be the permanent type of conversion, the expression of existing measurements in metric language. A can of soup containing 10½ avoirdupois ounces will be marked 297 grams, but it will be the same can of soup, and there will be no confusion as to whether the 10½ refers to avoirdupois or liquid ounces. A 50-foot roll of wax paper may remain the same and be marked 15.24 meters—or, to preserve a round number, it may be less than one inch shorter to make it 15 meters.

Adaptation in terms of dual dimensioning may be applied to some consumer goods during an extended transition period. A man's shirt may be marked with dimensions in both inches and centimeters–16½:32/42:81—until such time as people no longer know what 16½:32 means.

The actual dimensions of some mechanical consumer goods will change if the product must co-ordinate with other items— the height of stoves is a case in point if the height of kitchen counters is changed. However, the kitchen sink will not change when it is manufactured to the metric system. A change to metric will have no apparent effect on such things as toasters, mixers, oil burners, electric motors, garden tools, lawn mowers, and many other consumer items for which dimensions are of no consequence. When metric language is adopted the lawn mower will cut a 48-centimeter swath instead of a 19-inch swath but it will be, so far as the user is concerned, the same lawn mower. Or, because of the reverence for round numbers, metric lawn mowers may be made in 50- and 60-centimeter widths instead of 19 or 24 inches.

Conversion will bring a change in food and other products that are sold by the pound, the quart, or the gallon. In some cases—bread and milk are examples—laws provide that commodities be packaged in quantities that are based on Customary units. These laws would presumably change to replace the pound with the kilogram and the quart with the liter.

A change to the liter is of little consequence; it is only 5 percent more than a quart. The kilogram, however, is too large to be a convenient unit for packaging most foodstuffs. In metric countries, the half-kilo, 500 grams, is the most frequently used unit. Since both the liter and the half-kilo are larger than their Customary System counterparts, there will be an increase in prices that will surely have an adverse psychological effect. The so-called "70¢ spread" will become a "77¢ spread." The amount of butter will increase proportionately, but this will not be too apparent to the eye and the housewife may view the change as a price increase without considering the compensating increase in quantity.

In sports, there will probably be a varied response to a change to the metric system. All international competition in track and field is in metric terms. This has been confusing for American athletes who do not know the metric system; Jesse Owens said that he did not know how fast he ran in the 1936 Olympics, he had no idea what the distances meant. For a time, several years ago, amateur track and field events in the United States were converted to metric, but were then changed back. Under a general adoption of the system, track and field events would probably be metric, with record books using both systems for many years so that old and new records might be compared.

In most court or playing-field sports adaptation will probably be the permanent response, keeping the same dimensions expressed in metric language. Significant changes in the dimensions of a baseball diamond would be unthinkable because of the effect on the game. The distance between bases will remain the same although the regulations may specify that this distance be 27.43 meters instead of 90 feet. The same is true of basketball, tennis, and other sports where a court or playing field is involved. An exception may be football. The yard is such an integral part of this game that a change to the meter—increasing the length of the field by about 10 percent—would surely cause an uproar; and merely adopting metric language would make the 10-yard measurement between lines 9.144 meters.

This may be one of those "crucial situations" for which Dr. Astin said that some solution must be found other than adoption of the metric system. A better instance of a crucial situation, for which an easier solution was found, was illustrated by an incident in England. Shortly after conversion planning started, the railroads asked the Metrication Committee, "What are we going to do about mileposts? If we change to kilometers every one will have to be relocated, and 60 percent more posts will be needed." When asked the purpose of the mileposts the railroads replied that they were essential to pinpoint accidents or the need for repairs; if a track walker found a defective switch he phoned in that it was located a half-mile past milepost 42 and a crew was sent there to fix it. The Board then proposed that the mileposts be left where they were but that the name be changed from milepost to "marker." A track walker could then phone in that a repair crew was needed halfway between marker 42 and 43. Similarly simple solutions may be found for other "crucial" problems.

In considering conversion to the metric system, the advantages to the economy and the impact on industry are receiving primary consideration; little attention has been paid to the effects in the public area. So far as the public is concerned, the advantages of conversion would probably not be of sufficient weight to justify a change if this were the only consideration. For those who know it, the Customary System is as satisfactory as the metric system for most measurements in daily life. True, the metric system is easier to learn and simplifies calculations, but these advantages might not warrant throwing out the familiar system and learning a new one. The man in the street would gain little from the change.

There will probably be some proposals, as there have been in England, that conversion be limited to industry and government while the public continues to use inches and pounds.

This, of course, does not make sense. It would mean that children would have to learn both systems—one for use at work and the other in their daily lives. Commodities would be measured by one system at the wholesale level and by the other in retailing. People would have to learn the metric system anyway to convert products made to round metric measurements to familar inch measurements. If postal regulations are changed to make the unit of first-class mail 30 grams instead of one ounce, anyone who mails a letter will have to know what 30 grams is.

Sooner or later *everybody* will have to learn the metric system. Although antimetrics make much of the tremendous confusion and difficulty that this will cause, other nations have found that the transition was relatively simple and painless. India reported that even illiterates were readily able to learn the new system. Publicity and advertising—forms of public education—have been developed to a fine art in the United States. When their techniques are applied to familiarizing the public with the metric system everybody will quickly learn as much of it as they need to know for daily life.

Teaching people to *think* metric is a different matter. Few adults will ever learn this completely. There was an amusing example of this at the last annual meeting of the Metric Association, a group that has been propagandizing the metric system since 1915. At the opening of the meeting, the president of the association displayed to the audience a measuring instrument that the organization was producing, which he called a "metric yardstick." Of course, there can be no such thing as a metric yardstick—the yard is not a metric unit. The object he was presenting was, simply, a meter stick. But the mind of the president was so conditioned to the familiar inch-pound units that he unconsciously used the word for the Customary equivalent when referring to the stick.

Regardless of any target date that may be set for adopting metric weights and measures, it is safe to say that the United States will not be fully converted to the system until two generations of children, yet unborn, have reached adulthood. The first generation, which will enter school starting in the late 1970's, will probably learn both systems, perhaps at about an equal level. They will be bilingual in terms of measurements. When they leave school they will use the metric system at work but may use the inch-pound system for some purposes in the home. The second generation will learn only the metric system in school and will undoubtedly consider any use of the archaic Customary units by their parents as an indication that the older generation is not "with it." A young adult who is reading this book may some day be asked, "Granddaddy, what was an inch? Mommy says that you would remember."

One final advantage of the metric system. The all-wise American parent of the future will not have to disclose his feet of clay when his offspring raises his head from his homework and asks, "Daddy, how many pecks are there in a bushel?"

# APPENDIX

## THE SIX BASIC METRIC (S.I.) UNITS

**Length—METER—m**

> The meter is defined as 1 650 763.73 wavelengths in vacuum of the orange-red line of the spectrum of krypton-86.

**Mass—KILOGRAM—kg**

> The standard for the unit of mass is a cylinder of platinum-iridium alloy kept by the International Bureau of Weights and Measures in Paris.

**Time—SECOND—s**

> The second is defined as the duration of 9 192 631 770 cycles of the radiation associated with a specified transition of the cesium atom.

**Temperature—KELVIN—K**

> The thermodynamic or Kelvin scale of temperature has its origin or zero point at absolute zero and has a fixed point defined as 273.16 kelvins.

**Electric Current—AMPERE—A**

> The ampere is defined as the magnitude of the current that, when flowing through each of two long parallel

wires separated by one meter in free space, results in a force between the wires of $2 \times 10^{-7}$ newton for each meter of length.

## Luminous Intensity—CANDELA—cd

The candela is defined as the luminous intensity of 1/600 000 of a square meter of a radiating cavity at the temperature of freezing platinum (2 042K)

Note: The LITER—1—was redefined at the General Conference on Weights and Measures in 1964 as exactly 1 000 cubic centimeters. Since the centimeter is not a basic S.I. unit the liter is not acceptable as a unit in the S.I. system. However, it is generally used as a metric unit of volume or capacity.

## SUPPLEMENTARY UNITS

Plane angle—RADIAN—rad
Solid angle—STERADIAN—sr

## THESE PREFIXES MAY BE APPLIED
## TO ALL UNITS

| MULTIPLICATION FACTORS | PREFIX | SYMBOL |
|---|---|---|
| $1\ 000\ 000\ 000\ 000 = 10^{12}$ | tera | T |
| $1\ 000\ 000\ 000 = 10^{9}$ | giga | G |
| $1\ 000\ 000 = 10^{6}$ | mega | M |
| $1\ 000 = 10^{3}$ | kilo | k |
| $100 = 10^{2}$ | hecto | h |
| $10 = 10^{1}$ | deca | da |
| $1$ | (*Units*) | |
| $0.1 = 10^{-1}$ | deci | d |
| $0.01 = 10^{-2}$ | centi | c |
| $0.001 = 10^{-3}$ | milli | m |
| $0.000\ 001 = 10^{-6}$ | micro | $\mu$ |
| $0.000\ 000\ 001 = 10^{-9}$ | nano | n |
| $0.000\ 000\ 000\ 001 = 10^{-12}$ | pico | p |
| $0.000\ 000\ 000\ 000\ 001 = 10^{-15}$ | femto | f |
| $0.000\ 000\ 000\ 000\ 000\ 001 = 10^{-18}$ | atto | a |

# EXAMPLES

One kilogram  =  1 000 grams

One milliliter  =  1/1 000 of a liter

One centimeter  =  1/100 of a meter

## DERIVED UNITS

| QUANTITY | UNIT | SYMBOL |
|---|---|---|
| Area | square meter | $m^2$ |
| Volume | cubic meter | $m^3$ |
| Frequency | hertz | Hz  ($s^{-1}$) |
| Density | kilogram per cubic meter | $kg/m^3$ |
| Velocity | meter per second | m/s |
| Angular velocity | radian per second | rad/s |
| Acceleration | meter per second squared | $m/s^2$ |
| Angular acceleration | radian per second squared | $rad/s^2$ |
| Force | newton | N  ($kg{\cdot}m/s^2$) |
| Pressure or stress | newton per square meter | $N/m^2$ |
| Kinematic viscosity | square meter per second | $m^2/s$ |
| Dynamic viscosity | newton-second per square meter | $N{\cdot}s/m^2$ |
| Work, energy, quantity of heat | joule | J  (N·m) |
| Power | watt | W  (J/s) |
| Electric charge | coulomb | C  (A·s) |
| Voltage, potential difference, electromotive force | volt | V  (W/A) |
| Electric field strength | volt per meter | V/m |
| Electric resistance | ohm | Ω  (V/A) |
| Electric capacitance | farad | F  (A·s/V) |
| Magnetic flux | weber | Wb  (V·s) |
| Inductance | henry | H  (V·s/A) |
| Magnetic flux density | tesla | T  ($Wb/m^2$) |

| QUANTITY | UNIT | SYMBOL | |
|---|---|---|---|
| Magnetic field strength | ampere per meter | A/m | |
| Magnetomotive force | ampere | A | |
| Flux of light | lumen | lm | (cd·sr) |
| Luminance | candela per square meter | cd/m² | |
| Illumination | lux | lx | (lm/m²) |

## COMMON EQUIVALENTS AND CONVERSIONS
*Approximate*

| | |
|---|---|
| 1 inch | = 25 millimeters |
| 1 foot | = 0.3 meter |
| 1 yard | = 0.9 meter |
| 1 mile | = 1.6 kilometers |
| 1 square inch | = 6.5 square centimeters |
| 1 square foot | = 0.09 square meter |
| 1 square yard | = 0.8 square meter |
| 1 acre | = 0.4 hectare * |
| 1 cubic inch | = 16 cubic centimeters |
| 1 cubic foot | = 0.03 cubic meter |
| 1 cubic yard | = 0.8 cubic meter |
| 1 quart | = 0.95 liter * |
| | |
| 1 gallon | = 0.004 cubic meter |
| 1 ounce (avdp) | = 28 grams |
| 1 pound | = 0.45 kilogram |
| 1 horsepower | = 0.75 kilowatt |
| Fahrenheit temperature | = 9/5c. + 32 |
| | |
| 1 millimeter | = 0.04 inch |
| 1 meter | = 3.3 feet |
| 1 meter | = 1.1 yards |
| 1 kilometer | = 0.6 mile |
| 1 square centimeter | = 0.16 square inch |

* Common term not used in S.I.

| | |
|---|---|
| 1 square meter | = 11 square feet |
| 1 square meter | = 1.2 square yards |
| 1 hectare * | = 2.5 acres |
| 1 cubic centimeter | = 0.06 cubic inch |
| 1 cubic meter | = 35 cubic feet |
| 1 cubic meter | = 1.3 cubic yards |
| 1 liter * | = 1.05 quarts |
| 1 cubic meter | = 250 gallons |
| 1 gram | = 0.035 ounce (avdp) |
| 1 kilogram | = 2.2 pounds |
| 1 kilowatt | = 1.3 horsepower |
| Celcius temperature | = 5/9(F.–32) * |

*Accurate to Parts Per Million*

| | |
|---|---|
| inches × 25.4 * | = millimeters |
| feet × 0.3048 * | = meters |
| yards × 0.9144 * | = meters |
| miles × 1.609 34 | = kilometers |
| square inches × 6.4516 * | = square centimeters |
| square feet × 0.092 903 0 | = square meters |
| square yards × 0.836 127 | = square meters |
| acres × 0.404 686 | = hectares |
| cubic feet × 0.028 316 8 | = cubic meters |
| cubic yards × 0.764 555 | = cubic meters |
| quarts × 0.946 353 | = liters |
| gallons × 0.003 785 41 | = cubic meters |

*Accurate to Parts Per Million*

| | |
|---|---|
| ounces (avdp) × 28.349 5 | = grams |
| pounds × 0.453 592 | = kilograms |
| horsepower × 0.745 700 | = kilowatts |
| Fahrenheit – 32 × 5/9 * | = Celcius |
| | |
| millimeters × 0.039 370 1 | = inches |
| meters × 3.280 84 | = feet |
| meters × 1.093 61 | = yards |

* Exact.

| | | |
|---|---|---|
| kilometers $\times$ 0.621 371 | = | miles |
| square centimeters $\times$ 0.155 000 | = | square inches |
| square meters $\times$ 10.7639 | = | square feet |
| square meters $\times$ 1.195 99 | = | square yards |
| hectares $\times$ 2.471 05 | = | acres |
| cubic centimeters $\times$ 0.061 023 7 | = | cubic inches |
| cubic meters $\times$ 35.3147 | = | cubic feet |
| cubic meters $\times$ 1.307 95 | = | cubic yards |
| liters $\times$ 1.056 69 | = | quarts |
| cubic meters $\times$ 264.172 | = | gallons |
| grams $\times$ 0.035 274 0 | = | ounces (avdp) |
| kilograms $\times$ 2.204 62 | = | pounds |
| kilowatts $\times$ 1.341 02 | = | horsepower |
| Celcius $\times$ 9/5 + 32 * | = | Fahrenheit |

* Exact

# INDEX